The Gourmet's Guide To Mixed Drinks

The Gourmet's Guide To

Mixed Drinks

Thomas Cowan

QUILL
New York 1984

A QUARTO BOOK

Library of Congress Catalog Card Number: 84-42598

ISBN: 0-688-02502-1

The Gourmet's Guide To Mixed Drinks
was produced and prepared by
Quarto Marketing Ltd.
212 Fifth Avenue, New York, N.Y. 10010

Editor: Naomi Black
Art Director: Richard Boddy
Designer: Mary Moriarty
Editorial Assistant: Mary Forsell
Cover Design: Liz Trovato
Cover Photograph: Maria Robledo
Illustrations: Kurt J. Wallace

Typeset by BPE Graphics, Inc.
Printed and bound in the United States by
Interstate Book Manufacturers, Inc.

First Quill Edition
1 2 3 4 5 6 7 8 9 10

ABOUT THE AUTHOR

Thomas Cowan is a freelance writer of diverse interests and
numerous credits. He has tended bar in a Memphis restaurant
(formerly a cotton warehouse) overlooking the Mississippi
River, taught humanities on a college level, published numerous articles, and is an award-winning poet. Among his previously published books are *Beyond the Bath: A Dreamer's Guide*
and *Great Kid's Rooms*. He is currently working on the book
Beyond the Kitchen, to be published in 1985. He holds a Ph.D.
in history and literature from St. Louis University.

EMPIRE
•BOOKS•

Phone Orders
Gladly Accepted!

CENTRE TOWN
240 Bank (at Lisgar)
236-2363
9-6 Mon-Wed, Sat
9-9 Thurs, Fri
12-5 Sundays

LINCOLN HEIGHTS
GALLERIA
2525 Carling Avenue
820-7023
9:30-6 Mon-Wed, Sat
9:30-9 Thurs, Fri

WE FEATURE MORE WAYS TO STRETCH YOUR BOOK-BUYING DOLLAR!

- *WE WILL NOT BE KNOWINGLY UNDERSOLD! IF A BOOK WE HAVE IN STOCK IS SELLING FOR LESS ANYWHERE ELSE IN TOWN, LET US KNOW AND WE'LL MATCH THE PRICE!*

- *DISCOUNT BESTSELLERS AT 25 % OFF LIST PRICE!*
- *EMPIRE DOLLARS! RECEIVE **EMPIRE DOLLARS** WHENEVER YOU BUY $25 or more. THE MORE YOU BUY, THE MORE YOU RECEIVE!*

- **5% Discount FOR Seniors** *EVERY MONDAY*

- *CAN'T FIND WHAT YOU'RE LOOKING FOR? WE'LL GET IT FOR YOU WITH OUR STATE OF THE ART SPECIAL ORDER SERVICE AT NO ADDITIONAL CHARGE!*
- *ASK ABOUT OUR HANDY LAYAWAY SERVICE*
- **GIFT CERTIFICATES** *FOR ANY AMOUNT*
- *DISCOUNTS AVAILABLE TO LIBRARIES & INSTITUTIONS*

CONTENTS

INTRODUCTION

The history of mixed drinks is shrouded in mystery, myth, wishful thinking, and just plain tall tales. The hard facts, like the hard liquor, are sometimes obliterated by human invention. Certainly thirsty human beings have been concocting drinks composed of alcoholic and nonalcoholic substances since ancient times. But the cocktail as we know it (or think we know it) seems to have been around only since Elizabethan times when Englishmen warmed their mulled wine in kettles over roaring fires to blend the spices, sugar, and fruit peels both to celebrate the winter festivals and to keep warm in the stately, though drafty, homes of England. Colonials in America brought English drinking customs with them, particularly in the British navy where a daily ration of grog was seldom turned down. A tankard of rum, doctored with molasses and lemon juice from the tropical isles that lured explorers southward during that era, could be imbibed either with hot water or strong tea. Either as royal navymen or buccaneers, these explorers roamed the western seas and imported ingredients and recipes, tested and tasted them, and made the necessary adaptations for the new American palate.

The accepted nutritional advice in colonial times strongly warned people against drinking water straight, the assumption being that natural waters in the New World contained new impurities for which the British had little resistance. Killing off the bacteria by adding a splash of gin or rum to the water was a healthful idea that intoxicated generations of settlers in North America. Both here and in England, the cultivated class sang the praises of public life that centered around the local tavern, which in its day served as a hotel, restaurant, chamber of commerce, and was the eighteenth century's version of the evening news program and local gossip column. For in the tavern society of the Enlightenment, newspapers were read by those who could read to those who couldn't, and both literate and illiterate toasted the good news and drank to forget the troubles of the day. As Samuel Johnson put it, "There is nothing which has yet been contrived by man by which so much happiness is produced as by a good tavern or inn."

Liquor also played a key role in colonial politics, particularly in the South where those "standing" for office would entertain the entire electoral district on their gracious lawns, usually in good weather, when the heat of the day required a copious supply of beverages. It is not uncommon to discover in

6

the personal campaign budgets of Washington and his compatriots a sizable entry for alcohol to appease the local voters. It has been estimated that Virginia politics cost elected officials a considerable number of gallons per vote.

The word *cocktail* entered the American lexicon at least by 1806, when a contemporary newspaper referred to a "cocktail" as "an excellent electioneering potion . . . composed of spirits of any kind, sugar, water, and bitters." It was also referred to as a "bittered sling" even by those who didn't lose the election. Where the word actually came from is lost in history and myth. Americanists like to attribute it to Betsy Flanagan, a tavernkeeper, who purportedly served Washington's French allies a mixed drink in their off-hours. She either stirred or decorated the glasses with tail feathers stolen from a rooster owned by a Tory neighbor down the road, and thus was born the American cocktail. Nevertheless, the very French troops who bent their elbows at Betsy's wayside inn may have already heard the term in a cognate form from their own Bordeaux region where the phrase *"Vive le coquetel!"* was uttered to express devotion to the *coquetel* or mixed drink made from wine and brandy. It wasn't too hard to slur the phrase into *"Vive le coq's tail!"*

> *Always carry a flagon of whiskey in case of snake bite, and furthermore always carry a small snake.*
>
> —W. C. FIELDS

Another version of the origin of the term comes from the world of horse racing and trading. Supposedly unscrupulous horse traders would give their old nags a strong shot of some potent spirit that would cause them to "cock their tails" and strut around as if indeed they were high-spirited. Unsuspecting buyers could not always distinguish "high-spirited" from "high on spirits," and so many a race was won or lost. Others claim that the term came up the Mississippi River with boatmen who challenged one another to become the "cock of the walk," meaning the orneriest, meanest, cussedest rascal and wrestler on the River. It was a title that carried some weight in the feisty, two-fisted society that worked the docks, flatboats, and wharves of the river towns. Whoever was lucky enough to survive the ordeal to win the title was granted the right to wear bright red rooster plumage in his broad-brimmed hat, thus announcing to the world that he could outdrink, outfight, and outclaw anyone around.

Perhaps, too, the term came from some anonymous pirate sailing the seven seas in the Caribbean, where he indulged in the exotic drinks that were offered him in tribute and were garnished with brilliantly colored feathers of tropical birds. No one will ever know.

In the nineteenth century a concerted band of zealots was less interested in the origin of cocktails than in their results, particularly among the lower working classes who substituted straight whiskey and beer for the fancy cocktail. The temperance movement was in full swing by mid-century, counties went dry, and voters staggered to the polls on election day to keep their citizenry moral. For several generations many people continued to "vote dry and drink wet." The movement caught national approval during World War I, and the Prohibition Amendment was passed. The soldiers who fought in Europe to make the world safe for democracy returned home to discover that America was now safe from demon rum.

And so the war was on, fought out in the underworld of organized crime dominated by Al Capone and Al Cohol. It was the Jazz Age, an era of speakeasies, bootlegging (even the White House had its unofficial bootlegger), and bathtub gin. Actually, closing the saloons and taverns was a mixed blessing. Formerly the haunts of men, the saloons and taverns were considered off limits to most women. The only kind of woman seen there was "that kind of woman." Once closed, the local drinking establishments reopened as "cocktail lounges" known as speakeasies. The sawdust, swinging doors, and bawdy paintings behind the bar were replaced with plush carpets, velvet cushions, and sweet drinks to satisfy the New Woman who could now vote and drink. Ordering drinks became respectable, although illegal, for genteel women.

Because the illegal bootleg "stuff" tasted so bad, bartenders' wits were strained to concoct drinks that camouflaged the harsh taste of bootleg whiskey. Harry Craddock, a bartender who learned his trade at the Savoy Hotel in London, brought to America his knowledge and skill and promoted the new drinks among a populace anxious to join the local Bombay Bicycle Clubs for their so-called health conscious "activities." The noble experiment in legislated morality failed but not before it turned on a generation of American drinkers to the joys of finely wrought cocktails. Indeed, many of the classic cocktails we enjoy today had their origins in that era and gave birth to a rack of offspring. Recently the New York Bartenders Guild acknowledged over 10,000 mixed drinks; and as in the Twenties, there must be countless more that have never surfaced from the poolsides and patios of middle America where they were invented and imbibed.

The term "cocktail" is still undergoing transformations as are the many mixed drinks the term signifies. Today "cocktail" has become a rather generic word for any mixed drink. But originally its meaning was limited to an aperitif: a short, tangy, sour drink served before meals and based on a hard liquor such as bourbon, gin, or rum. Now a cocktail can refer to a drink of any size, taste, or ingredients, including long drinks that are technically highballs.

What is—or was—a classic cocktail? An authentic cocktail was made of at least two ingredients but often had three or more: the base liquor, the modifying agent or aromatizer, and the special flavoring and coloring agents. In other words, bourbon on the rocks did not qualify.

The base liquor ideally should comprise 50 percent of the drink. Some bartenders argue for as much as 75 percent of the total cocktail—the point being that the base alcoholic flavor should really predominate. It should not be drowned out by other ingredients.

The modifying agent or aromatizer was added to smooth and subdue the harsh bite of the straight liquor. These ingredients add an interesting character of their own to the drink and each brings out a different aspect of the original base liquor. Typical modifying agents include the aromatic wines such as vermouth and Dubonnet, bitters, fruit juices, sugar, cream, and eggs. As you learn drink recipes, you can experiment with the modifiers, altering amounts and substituting similar ones, to develop your own method of mixing drinks and inventing new ones.

Many cocktails have a third or fourth ingredient commonly referred to as the special flavoring and coloring agents. These are usually liqueurs, fruit syrups such as grenadine and orgeat, and fruit juices. Often these additional components are the same as modifying agents in other drinks. You can tell the modifiers from the flavoring and coloring components because the latter are usually added in small amounts, such as dashes, drops, and half teaspoons.

For example, in a Manhattan, bourbon is the base liquor, which is softened by the vermouth, the modifier, to which a flavoring agent of one or two drops of bitters is added. A Whiskey Sour is composed of bourbon as the base spirit, modified by lemon juice and flavored with a little sugar.

Tall drinks which are technically highballs, not cocktails, include a topper or mixer such as tonic, soda, or another carbonated beverage. Even fruit juice has become popular as a mixer rather than as a modifying agent, in such drinks as Screwdrivers, Cape Codders, and Greyhounds. But if you reduce the amount of juice or carbonated mix in drinks like these, you'll have a short version of these highballs, and they'll more closely resemble a classic cocktail. Just use a shorter glass and lessen the amount of mixer until it is less than 50 percent of the drink.

If there is any lesson to be learned from history it is probably that human beings don't usually learn much from history. If there is any lesson to be learned from the history of cocktails and mixed drinks it is that the world is always ready for a new drink idea even though many people stay loyal to the same drink for years and years. The 10,000-plus mixed drinks are just for starters, as are the 300-plus drinks explained in this book. Consider the recipes here merely as guidelines to be experimented with rather than as blueprints to be slavishly followed. For in the final analysis, the success of a good mixed drink is not in the ingredients themselves or how they are prepared and served, but, to paraphrase Samuel Johnson on the virtues of taverns, on how much happiness they produce. And on that point, only you and your guests can be the judge.

I must get out of these wet clothes and into a dry martini.
—ROBERT BENCHLEY

BASIC STOCK

If you have been mixing drinks at home for some time, you undoubtedly have many of the basic stock items in your bar already. If you're just beginning to build up a supply of liquor and cocktail paraphernalia, you may be wondering which of the countless brands, types, categories, colors, and flavors you should procure first in order to get started. Obviously, you probably won't go out and buy everything immediately. A well-stocked bar represents a sizable investment and is usually the result of months, even years, of learning what you and your friends generally like to drink. Supplies vary by season too, as do favorite drinks. For some people, Gin and Tonic is a summer drink, while Manhattans are for winter. Certainly, a Hot Toddy sounds wrong for August as would a Vodka Cooler in February. Nevertheless drinkers are a varied and unpredictable lot, and bartenders by nature and tradition should be accommodating.

But given the limitations of budget, space, and seasonal preferences, what are the essential items to get your bartending off to a good start?

Here are my suggestions:

Base Liquors

The basic ingredient in a cocktail is the base liquor; so to satisfy any request, you should have a bottle of each of the following:

rum, bourbon, Scotch, gin, vodka, and tequila.

You'll discover that a mixed drink usually does not require the finest brand. Very few so-called connoisseurs of Zombies, for instance, to use a somewhat outlandish example, really can tell the difference between a Zombie made with cheap rum and one made with the very finest. But even with simpler, less complicated drinks, such as Whiskey Sours, the average drinker does not appreciate a sour made with expensive bourbon any more than one made with a cheaper brand. On the other hand, if you are preparing a drink straight, on the rocks, or with only a splash of water, your guest will be able to tell the cheap brands from the more expensive ones. Eventually you may want to get two brands, one cheap and one expensive, of each of the liquors that people drink neat or with a splash of water, such as bourbon and Scotch. Gin drinkers, especially Martini aficionados, can detect the quality of gin when it is mixed with vermouth or tonic. So you should have a quality brand of gin on hand too. When you come right down to it, aficionados of any stripe know their pet spirit, so you may sooner or later keep one cheap and one expensive brand of each type on hand.

You should also have a bottle of red wine, white wine, and a grape-based brandy, such as Christian Brothers or Napoleon, for drinks that call for brandy as a flavoring agent. Similarly, keep a high quality brandy, such as cognac, for occasions when it is asked for straight.

Mixes

Many cocktails call for a simple mixer, such as the following:

soda, tonic, coke, 7-Up, and ginger ale.

These can be kept on hand in the refrigerator. Of course, they can't be kept too long in the refrigerator once they have been opened, because they will go flat. It's nearly impossible to predict the shelf life of mixes. Some can be opened, recapped, and stored for a long time without going flat. Others seem to lose their punch almost overnight. A way to test old bottles of tonic and soda is to open them, place your thumb over the top, and shake the bottle two or three times. Remove your thumb and look for bubbles. If there are none or very few, the mix is flat and shouldn't be used.

Mixers that will have to be purchased especially for your parties because they tend to go sour when kept too long are:

orange juice, pineapple juice, grapefruit juice, tomato juice, and heavy cream.

If you don't have to make fruit juice cocktails in great quantities, you should squeeze juice from fresh fruit whenever possible. (By this I mean cocktails requiring a teaspoon or tablespoon or one measure of juice, not the drinks that are basically a liquor over ice and filled to the top with juice, such

The whiskey on your breath
Could make a small boy dizzy;
But I hung on like death:
Such waltzing was not easy.
—THEODORE ROETHKE

as Screwdrivers and Cape Codders. These drinks, of course, should be made with "store-bought" juice.) Many home bartenders at first think squeezing oranges and limes is an aggravating task that goes unnoticed and unappreciated. But believe me, it makes a difference. Try fresh juice in a drink for yourself and you'll see what I mean. And should your guests not notice and not appreciate the effort, remind them of it! Once they are told, it will be impossible for them *not* to mention how much better a drink tastes with fresh fruit!

Brandies and Liqueurs

You'll find there are some drinks that call for the most esoteric type of brandy or liqueur, the type you'll probably never use again except in that drink. Everyone's bar has a bottle of something or other that hasn't been opened in ages. It's usually the bottle with the faded label, the sticky neck, and the cap or cork that can't be removed. It also tends to be shoved to the back of the cabinet or bar shelf.

But here are some brandies and liqueurs that are fairly common and are used in a good number of cocktails:

> *Christian Brothers brandy, cherry brandy, apricot brandy, triple sec or Cointreau, white and dark crème de cacao or Kahlúa, white or green crème de menthe, amaretto, Galliano, and of course sweet and dry vermouth.*

Garnishes

Most garnishes, especially fruit, will have to be bought for the occasion. The following, however, might be kept on hand in the refrigerator:

> *olives, pearl onions, and maraschino cherries.*

Other Ingredients

In addition to all of the above, a well-stocked bar should have:

> *sugar (either powdered or super fine) or sugar syrup, grenadine, bitters, salt, Tabasco sauce, and Worcestershire sauce.*

Many drinks call for a sweetener such as sugar or sugar syrup (sometimes called simple syrup). Large granulated sugar such as you put on cereal in the morning should never be used

> *The first glass for myself,*
> *the second for my friends,*
> *the third for good humor, and*
> *the fourth for mine enemies.*
> —JOSEPH ADDISON

> *It smells like gangrene starting in a mildewed silo, it tastes like the wrath to come, and when you absorb a deep swig of it you have all the sensations of having swallowed a lighted kerosene lamp. A sudden violent jolt of it has been known to stop the victim's watch, snap his suspenders and crack his glass eye right across.*
>
> —Definition of *corn licker* given to the Distillers' Code Authority
> IRVIN SHREWSBERRY COBB

since it is difficult to dissolve. Always use "superfine" sugar or powdered sugar since these blend more easily. You should, of course, use the coarser granulated sugar for rimming a glass.

Some bartenders prefer to use simply syrup instead of sugar since it is even easier to add and dissolve. The problem is that most recipe books give the amount in terms of fine or powdered sugar, so you will have to experiment to learn the equivalent in simple sugar.

Here is a recipe for making simple or sugar syrup.

> *Take three cups of sugar and one cup of cold water and combine over a high flame. Bring to a boil for a few minutes. Remove from the flame and allow to cool. Bottle it tightly. Sugar syrup will keep almost indefinitely.*

HOW TO PREPARE GARNISHES

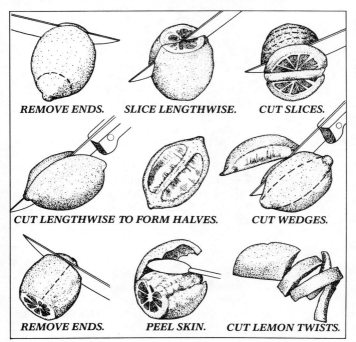

REMOVE ENDS.   SLICE LENGTHWISE.   CUT SLICES.

CUT LENGTHWISE TO FORM HALVES.   CUT WEDGES.

REMOVE ENDS.   PEEL SKIN.   CUT LEMON TWISTS.

BAR EQUIPMENT

Ironically, almost any drink could be made *without* most of the following items. In fact, many people find suitable substitutes for almost all of this equipment just by ransacking the kitchen. Nevertheless, half the fun of bartending is having the right paraphernalia that provides the professional touch. And let's face it, no matter what the job, if you don't have the right tools, it becomes aggravating. It is also true in mixing cocktails. The list below may look foreboding, but to anyone who takes the fine art of mixing drinks seriously and wants to prepare professional looking cocktails, the list is a must.

shot glass	*corkscrew*
speed pourers	*pitcher*
shaker	*ice crusher and scoop*
strainer	*paring knife*
bar spoon	*cutting board*
muddler	*juice squeezer*
ice bucket	*swizzle sticks*
tongs	*straws*
blender	*wiping clothes*
bottle opener	*coasters*

You'll find after mixing drinks for a while with the professional's equipment that a drink thrown together with improvised materials just isn't the same. You won't derive the same satisfaction from it, nor will your guests appreciate the fine skill and showmanship that goes into making a perfect cocktail. A good bar supply store in town should have all of these items. There are kits that contain the essential ones and are not too expensive. On the other hand, you could purchase each item separately. Depending on how elaborate or simple your home bar setting is, you can select most of these articles from a wide range of styles, prices, and quality, from plain to fancy, from cheap to expensive.

> *Some American writers who have known each other for years have never met in the daytime or when both were sober.*
>
> JAMES THURBER

As with equipment, the same with glasses. For the occasional party or happy hour, almost any glass will do. I'm sure you've drunk wine out of old-fashioned glasses and beer out of wine glasses at someone's home sometime or other. Not everyone can stock the proper size and shaped glass for every drink. You'll notice that even in commercial establishments, bar managers have simplified the glass scene by limiting the choice of glass to three or four basic ones. I worked in a bar where every drink, no matter what, was served in one of two glasses—a big one or a little one. Even draft beer and wine—always in a big one of course!

> *For a bad hangover take the juice of two quarts of whiskey.*
> EDDIE CONDON

Nevertheless, when drinks were invented, the originators usually had some special glass in mind to enhance the attractiveness of the drink. Consequently, certain glasses are now associated with certain types of drinks, and it has become de rigueur to serve them in their proper glass. If you want your own bar to be ready for any type of drink that is called for, here is a glass list:

    stem cocktail glass (4 oz)
    old-fashioned or rock glass (6 oz)
    highball glass (8 oz)
    collins glass (10 oz)
    sour glass (6 oz)
    wine glass
    liqueur glass
    champagne glass (flat saucer-shaped and tulip-shaped)
    snifter
    whiskey shot glass
    beer stein
    fireproof glass mug with handle or holder

Since in these more informal, if less genteel, times, it is rather arbitrary what type of glass is used with what type of drink, you should have some basic principles in mind when reaching for a glass.

For example, the size of the glass should correspond to the size of the drink. You would not want to serve a Martini, which is about four ounces of drink, in a collins glass. You'd have a very lonesome looking six ounces on top of the drink. Lonesome and empty. Similarly, if a drink recipe calls for you to "top the drink with soda," the size of the glass suggested in the recipe then becomes crucial for determining the right amount of soda. An old-fashioned glass would only let you "top" a four-ounce drink with two ounces of soda which would not be enough if the recipe calls for a highball or collins glass.

Often you'll discover a personal preference for how much topping beverage you like with various drinks. You might then want to change the size of the glass to accommodate it. For example, soda, tonic, ginger ale, or any other beverage will dilute the taste of the basic ingredients. If you find a particular drink too strong, sweet, bitter, fruity, or whatever and the drink calls for "top with soda," try a larger glass and increase the amount of soda. Also, you will have guests who may ask for a drink either short or long, meaning in a small glass or a tall one. Their own preferences are usually dictated by how strong they like the drink.

Another point to keep in mind concerns the difference between serving the same drink "up" (without ice) or "on the rocks" (with ice). If you are serving a simple four-ounce cocktail "up" you should always use the stemmed four-ounce cocktail glass. The same drink served "on the rocks" should go

BASIC BAR EQUIPMENT

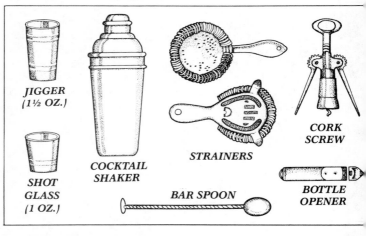

JIGGER
(1½ OZ.)

SHOT GLASS
(1 OZ.)

COCKTAIL SHAKER

STRAINERS

BAR SPOON

CORK SCREW

BOTTLE OPENER

BASIC BAR GLASSES

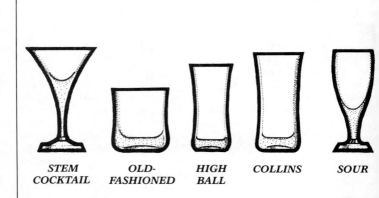

STEM COCKTAIL

OLD-FASHIONED

HIGH BALL

COLLINS

SOUR

> *Anybody that can't get drunk by midnight ain't trying.*
>
> TOOTS SHOR

into a six-ounce old-fashioned glass with two or three ice cubes.

A drink that is meant to be colorful should be served in a clear glass. Avoid the tinted or monogrammed glasses that would interfere with seeing the drink in its true colors. If you plan to serve these fancy neon drinks regularly, you should invest in clear glassware at the start. Otherwise you will have to have duplicate glasses, tinted for simple drinks and clear for the more colorful ones.

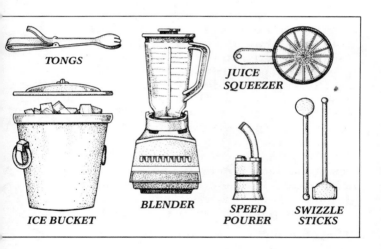

TONGS

JUICE SQUEEZER

ICE BUCKET

BLENDER

SPEED POURER

SWIZZLE STICKS

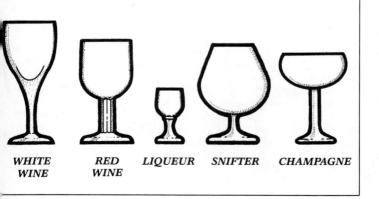

WHITE WINE

RED WINE

LIQUEUR

SNIFTER

CHAMPAGNE

TIME FOR DRINKS

If you listen to the likes of W. C. Fields any time is the right time for a drink. Less enthusiastic drinkers usually have their own notions of when to begin the afternoon happy hour and what hour in the morning it is proper to begin drinking. Even the day of the week or the season of the year may determine one's individual preferences. But when it is "time for drinks," what should you serve? In more traditional eras, there were certain drinks for certain occasions and times of the day or night. In the more relaxed and less formal age we now live in, the old guidelines are not adhered to very strictly. People experiment with any drink at any time. Nevertheless, folk wisdom and the human palate seem to suggest that there are certain drinks that hit the spot better at definite times and for definite occasions. Who wants (*really* wants!) hot wassail by the poolside in July? Or in a more subtle example, should you serve a creamy milk drink before dinner? Or how do you bridge the time from dessert to coffee to after-dinner drinks? And what will or will not put you to sleep as a nightcap?

The following suggestions are merely suggestions, arranged by time of day and season. None are de rigueur, the only unbreakable rule is to satisfy your guests. And to be charming, of course!

Morning

Late morning cocktail hours and brunches have grown in popularity in recent years so that people who never thought of having a mixed drink at 11:00 or before lunchtime, now find themselves having to plan a menu for a handful of guests who will expect a libation when they arrive. As with late afternoon and evening drinkers, there is a vast range of opinion on what is the best line of drinks for the morning hours. Some preferences have sound nutritional value to them, others are based purely on mystique.

Juice drinks such as Screwdrivers and Greyhounds and Cape Codders are favorites with many people because they are made of ingredients that one would ordinarily drink in the morning. Orange juice, grapefruit juice, cranberry or tomato juice have a tartness that perks one up physically and mentally. The various Bloodies (Bloody Mary, Bloody Maria, Bloody Bull) have more weight to them than the citric drinks and tend to be spicier which gets the slow movers moving. If you're looking for a real straight alcoholic beverage for a morning brunch, one you don't have to camouflage with breakfast juice, try champagne or a light brandy. Pernod and anise-flavored liqueurs have a sprightly licorice taste that can be invigorating in the morning hours. Or if you want the elegance of champagne blended with the wholesomeness of orange juice, serve Mimosas.

Many people come to brunches without having eaten breakfast and consequently down their first drink of the day on an empty stomach. For them, milk- or cream-based drinks will slow up the "buzz" that strikes many people too quickly when they drink on an empty stomach. Milk and cream coat the lining of the stomach and prevent the alcohol from rushing into the bloodstream (and to the head!) too fast. Milk and cream drinks are also soothing and substantial for people with a slight edge on their appetites. Banana Bliss, Pink Squirrel, Kahlúa Kiss, Golden Cadillac, and Brandy Alexander are satisfying morning cocktails as are others made with milk or cream and a liqueur.

> *So was their jolly whistle well y-wet.*
> —CHAUCER

Mid-Afternoon

People who have time to drink in the middle of the afternoon usually have a *lot* of time to drink in the middle of the afternoon. So if you plan to while away several hours chatting with a friend and sipping potent beverages, you should serve long drinks made in tall collins or highball glasses with lots of ice. Collins, coolers, tonics, and most drinks made with a base liquor and a carbonated or juice mixer allow you to drink slowly and languorously, and the fact that the ice keeps melting down and diluting the drink creates the illusion that you're doing "a lot of drinking" when in fact most of the time is spent twirling ice cubes around in a glass and sipping the insipid watery mixture. If you do actually refill the glasses several

> *What's drinking?*
> *A mere pause from thinking!*
> —LORD BYRON

times in the course of the conversation, you can begin to make them weaker since the liquor gets hidden anyway in many of the tall bubbly drinks. Your guests will appreciate you keeping them from getting too tipsy. Otherwise, they would never make it to cocktail hour.

> **The cocktail party—*a device for paying off obligations to people you don't want to invite to dinner.***
> CHARLES MERRILL SMITH

Cocktail Hour

There is no set time for the cocktail hour to begin. The practice seems to be that when work is over and the evening's relaxation can begin, people raise their glasses and toast the happy hour. For then they are truly happy. Traditionally the cocktail before dinner can be a long or a short drink in terms of size, but the guiding principle behind what kinds of liquors and mixes to serve is that the drink should not be too sweet or it will kill the appetite. The apéritif is therefore usually short and slightly sour or tart. The goal is to whet the appetite, not to kill it. Some people find long drinks to be too filling and for the same reason limit themselves to short drinks such as sours, martinis, manhattans, white wine, or a glass of dry sherry. Actually any vermouth-based cocktail makes a pleasant apéritif before a meal; its dry husky flavor stimulates the appetite and gets the mind into the right mood for a meal. The cocktail hour can last as long as you wish, keeping in mind your guests' hunger, but social customs suggest that you serve at least two rounds of drinks before announcing dinner is served. Two drinks relax the nerves, ease the mind, and usually loosen the tongue just enough for the stimulating conversation that will continue into the dinner hour.

After Dinner

Just as the apéritif should be tart or sour so as not to kill the appetite, the after-dinner drink should be sweet to cap off the meal. Most liqueur-based drinks, such as an amaretto or crème de menthe drink, provide the rich sweetness that complements the meal. A cream or egg drink is rich and smooth and can take the place of dessert itself or be served after dessert. A float is excellent for this: simply fill a liqueur glass about three-fourths full with your guest's favorite liqueur and then float heavy cream on top.

After or along with coffee, you might serve brandy straight or a rich brandy cocktail, such as a Brandy Alexander. Brandy or a liqueur mixed in coffee is also delicious after dinner.

Drinks made with Kahlúa or a coffee-flavored liqueur make nice transitions from coffee to the after-dinner hour. Either mix them yourself, or fill your guests' coffee cups about two-thirds full and present a tray of assorted brandies and liqueurs for them to select their favorites. A few empty liqueur glasses on the side will let them know they don't have to mix the spirit with the coffee.

Mists and frappés are cool, refreshing after-dinner drinks for people who like either liqueurs and brandies or those who want to return to their cocktail-hour liquor. A mist is made by pouring the spirit over crushed ice in a old-fashioned glass with a lemon twist. A frappé is practically the same drink but looks more elegant as it uses a stemmed cocktail glass. Heap the glass with crushed ice and pour the liquor over it. Serve with two short straws, no lemon twist. You can also make frappés in a blender. One jigger of liquor and about half a cup of ice will make a frosty and sturdy frappé.

> *There are two reasons for drinking:*
> *one is, when you are thirsty, to cure it;*
> *the other, when you are not thirsty, to*
> *prevent it. . . .*
> —THOMAS LOVE PEACOCK

The after-dinner drink par excellence is the pousse-café which literally means "to push down the coffee" (see Liqueurs). It's best to practice this one or any others before you attempt to serve it, since you need to know the specific densities of the various ingredients, get them in the right order, and have a steady hand in floating them on top of each other.

Before Bed

When the evening has come to a close and you're ready for bed, the nightcaps that best induce drowsiness are those made with milk or those served hot. Any hot toddy made with liquor, hot water, sugar, and a little lemon will do the trick. A favorite milk drink for bedtime is the Irish Cow.

Summer Drinks

People are naturally more thirsty in the summer than in the winter. The long hot days evaporate our bodily fluids more quickly, and we perspire and need to replenish them. Just the sight of a tall refreshing glass with beads of cold perspiration trickling down the outside is a reinvigorating experience. Pitchers filled with ice and punch. Tall collins glasses filled to the brim with sparkling refreshment and garnished with the fruits and berries of summer. It isn't hard to be a popular host or hostess for friends in the summer when the heat of the season makes most people less particular about what they want to drink. Anything tastes good so long as it is ice cold and there is plenty of it.

The obvious drinks for summer afternoons, picnics, and mid-day parties are the tall ones: coolers, collinses, highballs, and bucks. Particularly stimulating are wine coolers and punches made with white, red, rosé, or tingling champagne. Sangria can also hit the spot although some drinkers find it a little heavy. Still it's hard to beat the hefty pitcher of wine with pieces of apple and orange bobbing in it. Any tonic and lime cocktail will quench the driest thirst and perk up droopy spirits.

> *... a man hath no better thing under the sun, than to eat, and to drink, and to be merry...*
> —ECCLESIASTES 8:15

Here are some tips for making a hearty punch for a large number of guests, guidelines that will keep your punch fresh and plentiful with a minimum of effort (after all, if it's a hot day, you won't want to expend too much energy either!).

• *Prepare a batch of the basic ingredients and place them in the refrigerator to replenish the punch bowl when it begins to get empty. If the mix won't go bad unrefrigerated, you can keep it out, down by the pool or in the garden or patio close by so you don't have to run back to the kitchen.*

• *When the recipe calls for juice, use freshly squeezed juice rather than bottled juices since these have other additives (notably sweeteners) that can spoil the taste of the punch. Concentrated juices may not have the unwanted sweeteners, but read the label to see what the strength is and dilute it if necessary.*

• *Chill the punch bowl and all the ingredients before combining them so that the initial shock to the ice doesn't cause it to begin melting and diluting your punch too rapidly.*

• *A large block of ice will melt less quickly than ice cubes and is preferable if the party is outdoors where it will be hot. But even in an air-conditioned room, you may find that ice cubes weaken the punch.*

• *Any carbonated or bubbly ingredient such as champagne or soda should be added last, immediately before serving, so that the guests' first encounter with the punch is while it is still at its fizzy peak.*

• *Sugar is difficult to dissolve in cold liquids so use simple syrup rather than granulated or powdered sugar. Powdered or super-fine sugar will dissolve in a shaker, but there's no way you can shake a bowl of punch. Don't even try.*

• *When you make a punch containing tea, it's better to brew the tea with extra tea bags rather than to let it steep extra long. Too much steeping produces a strong bitter tea and the resulting tannic acidity can spoil the flavor.*

• *The amount of fruit pieces for a bowl of punch is a matter of taste and aesthetics. Some punches look as if they are meant to be eaten rather than drunk. A few pieces floating in the punch will suffice for atmosphere, the real flavor coming from their juices. On a hot day, however, it is nice to have a bowl of fruit nearby or a simple fruit salad if you really do want to have something to munch on.*

• *Regarding the amount to prepare, keep in mind that a gallon of punch fills about thirty-two punch cups (6 oz) and then estimate in terms of how many guests you are entertaining and how many cups they will probably want. A handy rule of thumb is that even light drinkers will probably want several cups on a hot day. Punch can be disarming too in that it's not always obvious at first how strong the mix is. Have extra on hand rather than let a guest come back only to find the bowl empty and his or her thirst irritable.*

Winter Drinks

Just as people are thirstier in the summer, so they tend to be hungrier in winter. Any winter cocktail party should include substantial nibbles or snacks. Traditionally satisfying winter drinks are any that are hot—hot toddies, hot spiced punch, hot milk drinks such as the Irish Cow, and hot cider concoctions. Hot tea laced with rum and any of the innumerable "coffees" hit the spot on a cold wintry day or evening. Brandy, whiskey, and rum are the base liquors that mix best in hot drinks. Try each in eggnog and notice the subtle differences among them. If you want a change from the usual hot drinks, try a flip such as a Sherry Flip or Brandy Flip. One egg, one teaspoon sugar, one and a half ounce of liquor, and a couple teaspoons of heavy cream. Shake well or put in the blender.

> *Crosspatch, draw the latch,*
> *Set by the fire and spin;*
> *Take a cup and drink it up,*
> *Then call your neighbors in.*
> —ANONYMOUS

When serving hot drinks, prewarm the mugs by pouring very hot water into them before filling. Mugs are best for hot drinks because your guests won't burn their hands on the handles. If you have heat resistant glassware, use a metal holder with a handle. Remember when refreshing a hot drink, don't just pour in more to the already lukewarm dregs. The result will still be a lukewarm drink. Empty the mug completely, rinse it in hot water, and then fill with a fresh drink.

HINTS FROM THE BARTENDER

When mixing drinks at home for your friends, you won't be expecting any tips as would a professional bartender mixing drinks for customers. Nevertheless, even best friends often watch your method of preparing their drinks as closely as they might watch a bartender at the cocktail lounge of a plush hotel. Style is as important as content. Mixing drinks is at least 50 percent vaudeville, or can be, with the proper flair, the deft flourish of the towel, the twist of the wrist, the dramatic way you pop the shaker from the glass.

Here are a few tricks of the trade to lend a dash of showmanship to your act. In addition, they will guarantee that you prepare the drink accurately.

> *Many a man who thinks to found a home discovers that he has merely opened a tavern for his friends.*
> —NORMAN DOUGLAS

Pouring

Of course you know how to pour liquor out of a bottle. You've been doing it for years! But how do you do it with style?

Assuming you are right-handed, hold the shot glass in your left hand and just to the left side of the mixing glass or drink glass so that the lips of the shot glass and the larger glass touch lightly. Then pour the liquor with your right hand so that when the shot glass just begins to overflow, you tip it smoothly into the mixing glass or drink glass. Generous bartenders usually then allow a little extra liquor to flow into the glass so that the customers know they are getting a little more than the exact measure. The extra splash won't hurt the flavor of most drinks, and friends and customers enjoy the privilege of getting a little more than they bargained for.

For a really professional looking pour, invest in a set of

speed pourers which you can purchase at a bar supply store or the gift and novelty section of a department store. These are the plastic spouts (sometimes metal) that you see on bottles behind the bar in a cocktail lounge. A speed pourer allows you to pour quickly in a narrow stream. In fact, there is so much control over your pour that you can grab the bottle with a flourish and invert it completely upside down as you direct the swift lean stream of liquor into the glass. With practice you can learn how long a pour equals one shot. Once you've got your "count" down, you won't need to use a shot glass for measuring the liquor. Seize the bottle, pour, and count.

Practice with a bottle of water. Count how long it takes to fill a one-and-a-half-ounce shot glass with a speed pourer. Yes, count. One...two...three...four...It doesn't matter how fast you count just as long as you count at the same speed each time. My count is a fast eight. Soon, you won't even have to count. You'll feel the count.

Most speed pourers fit snugly into the mouth of the bottle, but to make sure one doesn't fall out while you're pouring, always grasp the bottle by its neck so that your index finger is over the base of the speed pourer holding it safely in place.

If you have a bar where the bottles are left out and on display, such as they are in a commercial bar, the overall appearance is neater if you adjust the speed pourer to face left (for a right-handed bartender) when the bottle is on the shelf with its label outward. When all are lined up this way, you can see what each bottle is without turning it around and you can pick each one up, ready to pour. Place it back in its proper place and it's lined up with the others, ready for the next drink.

To Stir or To Shake?

Some drinks are stirred, some are shaken. How do you know which to do if the recipe doesn't say or you are making the drink from memory and can't remember. A handy rule is to stir drinks whose ingredients are light or clear and will blend easily, such as clear liquor bases with a light mix, like vermouth, tonic, or soda. Shaking is preferred for ingredients that are heavy in density or color and would not blend easily by stirring, such as cream drinks, juices, egg drinks, and cocktails calling for a syrupy liqueur.

There is great ritual and ceremony involved in stirring and shaking. Not only are there correct and incorrect ways of performing these feats, but it is by how smoothly they are executed that a bartender displays his or her style, flair, personality—or lack of them!

> **Q. *Were you drunk at four a.m.?***
> **Bogart: *Isn't everybody?***
> HUMPHREY BOGART

Stirring a Drink

After pouring the ingredients into the mixing glass along with
the ice, insert a bar spoon, and with the back of the spoon
touching the wall of the mixing glass, rotate it around the glass,
letting it twirl in your fingers so that the back of the spoon
stays against the glass. It's a little tricky at first, but you'll get it.
Stirring this way will make the ice spin in the middle of the
drink and, because it is a relatively silent method of stirring,
gives the impression that the ingredients are being mixed
without being unduly upset or bounced around. Martini drinkers, in particular, can be concerned about what they call
"bruising" the gin—an ailment gin will supposedly complain
about, but only martini drinkers can hear the gripe. Stir about
ten or twelve complete rotations. Too long a stir will dilute the
drink. Then remove the bar spoon, put the strainer in place,
and pour. The result is a clearer looking drink than one that is
shaken.

Shaking a Drink

Shaking produces a cloudier looking drink. Some drinks, such
as sours, should be cloudy. Shaking also creates fizz or foam for
drinks that require a little froth of one type or another. To
shake, first put the ice in the metal part of a Boston shaker and
add the other ingredients. Place the glass half into the metal
part slightly tilted. Do not insert the glass section straight up
and down or you will not be able to get the two apart! Tap the
glass gently on its bottom (still tilted of course) so that it fits
snugly. You don't want the two halves to fly apart during your
dramatic shake. Grab the shaker in both hands so that each
hand holds the bottom of its half. Raise the shaker to shoulder
level and shake vigorously forward and backward over your
right shoulder until the shaker feels cold, about ten times. As
with stirring, too long a shake will dilute the drink. Then pop
the two halves apart, lay the strainer across the metal half, and
pour.

Pouring a Mixed Drink

After stirring or shaking a drink, you then pour it into the glass
in which it will be served. Stirring and shaking accomplish two
goals: to mix the ingredients and to chill the drink. Even if the
drink is to be served over ice, a professional drink should
consist of fresh ice cubes, not the ones used to chill the drink in
the mixer or shaker. Therefore, place the strainer over the
mouth of the mixing glass, hold it in place with your index
finger, and strain the drink into the serving glass. Dump out
the used cubes, rinse the mixing glass or shaker, and you're
ready to prepare the next drink.

It may take practice and experience to mix a drink and pour
it into the proper sized glass with the right amount of ice so
that you don't end up with a drink that is too short (i.e., does

not fill the glass) or too long (i.e., overflows the glass). If you mix and pour too short, sometimes an extra ice cube or two will bring the drink level up to a respectable height. Another trick is to add a splash of soda which in small quantities will not adversely affect the taste or dilute the drink. If you have mixed too much, save it and after your guest has taken the first sip or two, add it to the glass, creating the illusion of magnanimously having offered him a refill unasked for! It too, like the fresh squeezed fruit juice, will be appreciated.

Muddling

Some drinks call for a cube of sugar, a berry, a mint leaf, or a piece of fruit and perhaps a splash of soda or a dash of bitters to be muddled in the glass before the base liquor and ice are added. A muddle is a wooden or metal stick with a bulbous end with which the ingredients to be muddled are crushed in the bottom of the glass. Tamping them several times with the muddler usually does the trick.

Frosting a Rim with Sugar or Salt

Drinks like Margaritas and Beachcombers are served in glasses with rims frosted with salt and sugar respectively. Rimming a glass with sugar or salt can be done in two ways. If the drink calls for a garnish such as a lemon, lime, or orange wedge, use a wedge of the fruit to moisten the rim of the glass before any of the ingredients or ice are added. Run the wedge around the rim. While still wet, dip the glass into a shallow saucer of salt or sugar as called for. Then set the glass aside while you make the drink. If garnish is not needed, keep a clean wet sponge sitting in a little dish of water. Place the glass upside down on the sponge, push it into the sponge, and—presto!—you have a glass rim wet and ready to be dipped. Unless a drink calls for rimming with powdered sugar, granulated sugar should be used because it crystalizes and stays hard on the rim.

Metric Conversion Table

To change	To	Multiply by
teaspoons	milliliters	5
tablespoons	milliliters	15
fluid ounces	milliliters	30
ounces	grams	28
cups	liters	0.28
pints	liters	0.47
quarts	liters	0.95
gallons	liters	3.8
pounds	kilograms	0.45

Chilling a Glass

Most cocktails are served cold. Hot drinks are the exception. Serving a cocktail in a chilled glass is a nice touch. If a refrigerator is handy, put the glasses in about thirty minutes before serving. About five minutes in the freezer will do. If you are not near a frig, before you start to prepare a drink, place ice cubes in the glass you intend to serve it in. The glass will chill while you mix the drink. When the cocktail is ready to be poured, dump the cubes out and pour the drink in. If you're serving a drink on the rocks, replace the partially melted cubes with fresh ones before pouring. You might think that no one would be able to tell the difference. Well, the truth is, no one can. We're not talking about deception. We're talking about the little touches on which civilization rests!

Frosting a Glass

If you want to serve a drink in a frosted glass, wet the glass before placing it in the freezer. If you have an extra refrigerator or deep freezer, you might want to keep a supply of glasses and beer steins frosted for unexpected occasions when an ice-cold drink in a frosted glass would hit the spot.

About Ice

Being an agile bartender means acquiring the skill of juggling ice. About 80 percent of the activity involved in mixing a drink concerns the manipulation of ice. There's no avoiding cold hands, but here are some tips for overcoming cold feet.

There's nothing more aggravating than to reach into the ice bucket with a pair of tongs, clamp them around a cube of ice, and discover that you're trying to pull out an iceberg. Ice has a way of sticking to itself, cube upon cube. You can prevent a certain amount of this sticking at the start when you take the ice cubes out of the tray by not running water over the ice to loosen the cubes. Wet cubes freeze to each other. Rather, let the tray sit for a few minutes after you take it out of the freezer, and then remove the cubes. They'll be drier this way and if you get them quickly into the bucket and covered before they begin to melt and get wet, there's less chance that you'll find them stuck in one unsightly and unmanageable clump.

Ice is put into the glass to keep the drink cold; it's not meant to dilute the drink. Yet that's what in fact happens, and there's no preventing it unless you happen to be serving cocktails at the North Pole. But here are some pointers to keep in mind to slow down the dilution. Ice cubes melt more slowly than crushed or shaved ice. Crushed ice melts the fastest; second is shaved or cracked ice. In general, the larger the chunk of ice the longer it will take to melt. This is important when making a large bowl of punch that you plan to last through most of the evening. One large cake of ice will melt more slowly than the same amount of ice in cubes. So for large punch bowls it's better to use a cake or block of ice rather than empty your ice trays into it.

The same principle is behind the suggestion that you never use the cubes for shaking or stirring a drink in the actual glass you plan to serve your guest. These cubes have already begun to melt in the mixing process and are on their way to becoming little slivers of ice. Hence, the practice of straining the drink into a glass filled with fresh ice cubes. Assuming the fresh cubes have been kept in a tightly closed ice bucket, they should be relatively dry and firm.

You can give the ice a little assist in its task of keeping the drink cold by chilling the mixer and any other ingredients that won't be spoiled by refrigeration. Obviously, mixes like soft drinks, tonic water, club soda, fruit juices, wine, vermouth, and others can be kept on ice before they are added to the drink. "On ice" is a literal suggestion if you can arrange it. A tub of ice can hold the mixers that you'll be using throughout the party. The refrigerator will work also, but you may not have one immediately at hand, and even if you do, it requires you going into the refrigerator each time you want to reach for the mixer. But however you arrange it, remember that chilled mixers will keep the drink cold, help the ice along, and keep it from melting down too soon and diluting the drink.

Hot Drinks

When serving hot drinks your goal is to keep the drink hot and not allow it to cool off or become lukewarm too quickly. Many drinks become almost impossible to swallow when lukewarm. You can retard the cooling off process by serving hot drinks in prewarmed mugs. Simply rinse the mug in hot water before pouring in the drink. Or if the mug is heat-resistant, pour very hot, almost boiling water into it and then empty it for the drink. If you serve very hot drinks in glasses that were not made to take a lot of heat, you can prevent them from cracking by placing a silver spoon in the glass before you pour in the drink. The metal will absorb the initial shock of the hot fluid and save the glass.

The question of "freshening up" a hot drink for a guest is perplexing. If there is still a considerable amount of the first drink in the glass, but it has cooled off to the point of not being worth drinking, it's best to make an entirely new drink. Adding more of the mixture, even though it is piping hot, will never bring the temperature back to the ideal one. The second drink will then cool off too rapidly, and you're back where you began with the drink needing to be freshened.

Floating an Ingredient

Some drinks suggest (or demand!) you float the final ingredient on top. Usually this is a high proof spirit or a particularly colorful liqueur. Floating is primarily for looks, although it also enhances the aroma and first sip by leaving the floated ingredient near the surface. Even if the floating ingredient eventually runs down into the drink (and most of them do, gravity being what it is) the initial effect is meant to be colorful and dramatic. The way to float a flavoring or coloring agent is to turn the bar spoon upside down and steady it by laying the stem on the rim of the glass. Carefully and slowly, pour the topping over the bowl of the spoon so that it cascades off the entire circumference of the spoon. The ingredient to be floated thus hits the surface of the drink in smaller, less concentrated quantities and at places equidistant from the center. A little practice (and perhaps a quick skim through your high school physics book) will give you the knack of it.

Adding a Twist

When a drink calls for a twist of lemon, lime, or orange, it means that a thin strip of peel should be twisted over the drink and dropped in. Here's how it's done. To prepare twists, take the fruit and cut off each end about one half inch from its tip. Then with a paring knife cut strips about a quarter-inch wide from one end of the fruit to the other, taking care that the knife cuts only the peel and not the pulp of the fruit on the inside. Once the fruit is striated with these incisions on all sides, peel back each strip, tearing it from the ball of the fruit which will eventually look bald and have no further use as a garnish. You can, however, squeeze it for the juice.

When adding a twist to a drink, take one strip of peeling between the thumb and index finger of each hand and twist it gently so that a small drop of oil emerges. You'll see the oil on the outside of the peel, not inside. Then rim the glass with the oily outer side of the peel and drop it in the drink. The oil on the rim of the glass will leave a tangy citric aroma and taste.

Squeezing a Wedge of Fruit

I won't insult you by telling you how to squeeze a wedge of lime or lemon, but if your guest is sitting rather close, watching you, it's a good idea to cup your free hand over the hand that is squeezing the wedge so that it won't shoot a spray of citric acid into your friend's eye. Citric fruit is perverse and always manages to hit the eye.

Sequence of Events

Chances are your guests won't scrutinize the way you prepare their drinks as much as they would in an expensive cocktail lounge where they hope the bartender is not going to pour "short" on the liquor, but they may watch you for style and flair. Is there any preferable sequence for mixing a drink? With some drinks, such as Martinis, you should never put the vermouth in before the gin. Everyone knows that. But should the ice go into a glass before the rum in a Rum and Coke? Does grenadine go in before the fruit or after? Does the garnish go in before the straw or vice versa?

Well, here are some suggestions.

Some home bartenders prefer to put the more expensive liquor ingredient in last (assuming there is no set sequence to a particular drink), because if they get distracted by conversation with their guest and ruin the drink before it's finished, they haven't wasted the liquor. Professional bartenders, who have nerves of steel and awesome powers of concentration, do it the other way. Here is the professional way:

1. *The base liquor goes into the mixing glass or shaker along with the ice, followed by the other ingredients in no particular order.*
2. *These are then stirred or shaken.*
3. *The drink is strained into a glass either with ice cubes or empty if the drink is called for "up."*
4. *Then, if the drink is a tall one, it is topped with soda or some carbonated beverage.*
5. *Next, the garnish goes on.*
6. *Last, a straw is inserted if the recipe calls for one.*

You'll notice in most recipes, especially ones that can go in a blender, the order of ingredients is never important. What is important is to read the recipe carefully because not all ingredients go in at the same time. Some drinks call for several of the ingredients to be mixed first, then the others added later.

Note: If the drink calls for a bubbly mix, such as champagne or a carbonated beverage, it should always go in as the last liquid ingredient and preceding the garnish. The reason is that when poured earlier, the mix begins to lose its effervescence and may have "bubbled out" before you actually serve the drink to your guest. Also, when stirring a drink to which you have just added a bubbly topper, don't stir too long or strenuously. A few gentle spins of the stirrer is sufficient. And one last and important point is not to put carbonated mixes, especially champagne, into a blender. They have a tendency to explode.

For drinks such as Rum and Coke or Seven and Seven (i.e., a drink that is primarily a base liquor topped with a nonalcoholic beverage in a tall glass filled with ice), the usual procedure is to fill the glass with ice, add the liquor, then fill up near to the top with the carbonated beverage, leaving room for a wedge of fruit and a little space to insert a swizzle stick and stir. The point here is that these types of drinks can dispense with the mixing glass and shaker. In general, Rum and Coke people are not as particular as Martini people, even though they might be the best of friends.

A woman drove me to drink and I never even wrote to thank her.

—W. C. FIELDS

BOURBON AND RYE

"Bourbon and branch" is the way they order it down South. Branch meaning spring water, of course. And just a splash, please. Or "bourbon on the rocks." Now you're talkin'! Today over 50 percent of the bourbon distilleries are in Kentucky where bourbon was first concocted in the eighteenth century. Bourbon County, Kentucky, some say. Some say not. But it was definitely the Revolutionary War generation, farmers whose ancestry went back to the British Isles, who brewed the hearty robust drink that epitomized the pioneer life on the American frontier, where corn replaced barley as a crop more suited to the fertile valleys and rolling hills. Out of the good earth, mineral waters bubbled up from Virginia to Missouri. Together, corn and spring water produced the corn mash that would eventually become the first truly American whiskey. One bourbon fan described the spring water with oratory that might equally describe the American pioneer spirit: the water came "leaping from rock to rock, laughing in its wild career until it found its haven of rest in the bosom of a mash tub." Wild, restless, productive, optimistic, searching for a home.

Although the term "bourbon" did not catch on until after the Civil War, "whiskey" as it was then called played a minor though significant role in early U.S. history. The famous—or infamous—whiskey tax levied by the Washington Administration in the 1790s raised once again the cry of "no taxation without representation" since western pioneer counties were notoriously under-represented in Congress due to the census takers never quite catching up with westward migration. Some settlers in Kentucky and Tennessee even threatened to secede from the Union. Of course no state would actually do that for another sixty-some years. But the idea was planted. The Whiskey Rebellion was quelled with 13,000 troops—more than Washington ever commanded at one time during the Revolution! They succeeded in catching two culprits in western Pennsylvania, dragged them back to the nation's capital in Philadelphia, where they were pardoned by Washington himself! But the point was made—the new government would be obeyed!

And over the years, some of those federal laws were written to regulate whiskey itself. By law, bourbon must be at least 51 percent corn mash (the rest comprised of barley and rye) and aged in charred oak barrels, which imparts the rich amber color and the earthy sweetness. Legend has it that the discovery of the wonderful things charred oak can do to whiskey was made by a distiller who intended to use barrels previously filled with fish. To eradicate the fish smell, he burned the insides. Maybe. At any rate, it was a fortuitous discovery.

Straight bourbon is made with sour mash, meaning that a residue from a previous distillation is added to the current one, to provide consistency. A sweet mash is totally fresh yeast. Straight bourbon should be aged for at least four years.

Corn whiskey must be 80 percent corn and should be aged in uncharred kegs for two years. A drink most prevalent in rural areas, it packs a whallop with its harsh, bitter taste, and its cussed potency. In folklore, backwoods drinkers often preferred it fresh off the still, and advertisements for one brand stated "less than 30 days old." Young, yes, but clearly not a babe-in-the-woods.

Rye, as you might guess, is at least 51 percent rye, the rest being other grains. Canadian whiskey is often called "rye" from olden days when it was primarily rye. Today Canadian distillers use corn, wheat, barley, and other grains, but the term rye has stuck so that some people mistakenly think all Canadian whiskey is rye. Of course, there is a bona fide Canadian rye and so stated on the label, but the term is applied loosely to other whiskeys as well, which tend to be lighter bodied than American whiskey.

"Blended" whiskeys were promoted during World War II when wartime allocation of grain threatened the whiskey industry. In order to stretch the amounts of straight whiskey available, distillers blended it with other grains. By law, at least 20 percent of a blended whiskey must be straight whiskey distilled at 100 proof; the rest consists of neutral, unaged spirits. The result is a lighter whiskey that adapts well to mixed drinks. By themselves, however, they often lack a distinctive character compared to the more assertive straight brands.

❖ ALGONQUIN ❖

Here's a drink for those with literary aspirations, named after the famous Algonquin Room in the Algonquin Hotel in New York City where literary greats and near-greats have sat for several generations, spinning out tales and yarns, some of which became great literature. The round table is still there where William Dean Howells held court in the late nineteenth century and determined the literary tastes for a nation.

2 oz rye
1 oz dry vermouth
1 oz pineapple juice
Shake with ice and serve up or on the rocks.

❖ ALLEGHENY ❖

The Allegheny is the perfect drink for bourbon lovers who have that bottle of blackberry brandy they just can't seem to get rid of!

1½ oz bourbon
1 oz dry vermouth
1½ tsp blackberry brandy
1½ tsp lemon juice
Lemon twist
Shake with ice, and serve up in a cocktail glass or on the rocks in an old-fashioned glass. Twist the lemon peel and drop into the drink.

❖ CANADIAN COCKTAIL ❖

This drink, and the following one, can be made with bourbon or rye if you don't have Canadian whiskey.

1½ oz Canadian whiskey
1½ tsp triple sec
1 tsp sugar
Dash of bitters
Shake with ice, and strain into a cocktail glass or over ice in an old-fashioned glass.

❖ CANADIAN SUNSET ❖

Who would have thought that the rising and setting sun would provide the names for two favorite drinks in North America, one coming from Canada, the other, the Tequila Sunrise, coming from Mexico?

2 oz Canadian rye or bourbon
1 oz Galliano
1 oz Strega
2 oz lemon juice
Couple dashes of Angostura bitters
1 tsp grenadine
Pour the grenadine into an empty cocktail glass. Shake all other ingredients with ice and strain into the glass. Do not stir.

❖ DAISY ❖

Daisys can be made with virtually any liquor. The basics are the lemon juice, sugar, and grenadine. There's even a Chocolate Daisy which does not have chocolate in it but rather equal parts of brandy and port. A Daisy without the grenadine, of course, is a Collins.

1 ½ oz bourbon
Juice of ½ lemon
½ tsp sugar
1 tsp grenadine
Soda
Orange slice, cherry, or raspberry
Shake bourbon, lemon juice, sugar, and grenadine with ice. Strain into a stein, metal tankard, or sour glass. Add one cube of ice. Top with soda. Garnish with fruit.

❖ DIRTY SINK ❖

Some people call this a Depth Bomb or a Depth Charge, but don't confuse the latter with the brandy cocktail of the same name. Basically, Dirty Sinks and the Depth "Drops" are shots of whiskey sunk into a stein of beer. Yes, shot glass and all. There's no real trick to making this. The tricky part is the last swallow or two. Be careful or the shot glass slides down the side of the beer stein and cracks you across the bridge of your nose.

Beer
1 shot bourbon
Fill the beer stein half full with beer. Lower a shot glass of bourbon into it. Fill the stein rest of the way.

❖ EVERYBODY'S IRISH ❖

At least that's what they say on St. Patrick's Day. Bourbon, of course, is not Irish, but it wears enough green in this concoction that it could possibly pass as a son—or a daughter—of Erin.

2 oz Irish whiskey or bourbon
1 tsp green Chartreuse
1 tsp green crème de menthe
1 green olive or 1 green cherry
Stir with ice and strain into a cocktail glass. Suspend the olive or cherry in the drink.

> *Give an Irishman lager for a month, and he's a dead man. An Irishman is lined with copper, and the beer corrodes it. But whiskey polishes the copper and is the saving of him.*
> —MARK TWAIN

❖FRISCO SOUR❖

2 oz bourbon
Juice of ¼ lemon
Juice of ½ lime
1 oz Bénédictine
Lemon and lime slices

Shake ingredients with ice and strain into a sour glass. Garnish with lemon and lime.

❖GLOOM LIFTER❖

The fact that this recipe calls for Irish whiskey is not meant to imply that the Irish are more prone to gloom than other nationalities, although there is certainly a mournful strain through many an Irish air. Substitute Kentucky bourbon when it's gloomy time down South. There is a gin drink called a Gloom Raiser which may raise your spirits in London, if not the fog. And a Gloom Chaser, made with Grand Marnier, may help you romp your way through a Gallic glump.

2 oz Irish whiskey or bourbon
Juice of ½ lemon
1 tsp sugar
½ egg white

Shake all ingredients well with ice and strain into a cocktail glass. For a pleasant variation add a teaspoon of brandy.

❖HIGHBALL❖

Here it is—the drink whose name is becoming almost a generic term for cocktail or mixed drink. In fact, because the filler can be almost any carbonated beverage, you should ask your guests specifically what they would like in it. Traditionally, however, the Highball was simply bourbon and soda.

1½–2 oz bourbon
Soda

Pour the bourbon over three or four ice cubes and fill with soda. Once around with a stirrer and the drink is ready. Other carbonated fillers may be used, such as 7-Up, ginger ale, etc.

❖IRISH COFFEE❖

The original liquor-in-coffee drink. Now you'll find all sorts of national and ethnic coffees: Jamaican, Mexican, Italian, to name but a few. And some people even add a coffee liqueur to this concoction. But to authentic and inauthentic Irishmen, Irish whiskey and coffee is preferred because some kind of "magic" happens when the two are mingled together. If you can't taste it, then perhaps you're neither type of Irishman!

1½ oz Irish whiskey
Sugar
Coffee
Whipped cream

Use either a stemmed glass or a cup. Some people like the glass or cup rimmed with sugar; others prefer the sugar put in the bottom. Add the whiskey and fill to within a half inch with hot coffee. Float the whipped cream on the surface carefully so that it rides there as you serve the drink.

❖IRISH COW❖

This drink makes an efficient nightcap when you really want to doze off and have a good night's sleep. A variation on this drink utilizes rum instead of Irish whiskey and has nutmeg sprinkled on the top.

1½ oz Irish whiskey
1 cup hot milk
1 tsp sugar

Heat the milk and pour it into a highball glass and then stir in the sugar until it is completely dissolved. Add the whiskey and stir gently.

❖JOHN COLLINS❖

Collins, Daisys, and Sours come from the same family of drinks, each being a variation on the other, but only the Collins branch of the family bothered with first names. Here's Johnny!

2 oz bourbon or rye
Juice of ½ lemon
1 tsp sugar or syrup
Soda
Orange and lemon slices and cherry

Shake whiskey, lemon juice, and sugar with ice. Strain into a collins glass and add several ice cubes. Top with soda. Give it a stir with a long straw and garnish with fruit.

❖KENTUCKY COLONEL❖

2 oz bourbon
2 tsp Bénédictine

Stir with ice and strain into an old-fashioned glass filled with ice.

❖KLONDIKE COOLER❖

2 oz Canadian whiskey
½ tsp sugar
2 oz soda
Ginger ale
Orange or lemon spiral

Muddle the sugar and soda in a collins glass. Fill with ice and add whiskey. Top with ginger ale and stir once more. Dangle the orange or lemon spiral over the rim of the glass and serve.

❖LADIES COCKTAIL❖

As Michael Jackson suggests, the name for this cocktail may have been due to bartenders' (traditionally male) prejudices.

2 oz bourbon
½ tsp Pernod
½ tsp anisette
Couple dashes of angostura bitters
Pineapple slices

Stir bourbon, Pernod, anisette, and bitters with ice, and strain into a cocktail glass. Garnish with a slice or two of fresh pineapple.

❖ LOS ANGELES ❖

1½ oz bourbon
Dash of sweet vermouth
1 tsp sugar
1 egg

Shake with ice and strain into a cocktail glass. For a slightly tarter variation, try adding the juice of half a lemon.

❖ MANHATTAN ❖

1½ oz bourbon
¾ oz sweet vermouth
Dash of bitters
Cherry

Stir the bourbon, vermouth, and bitters with ice and strain into a cocktail glass. Some people prefer the bitters left out altogether, or dashed into the drink after it is poured. If ordered on the rocks, use an old-fashioned glass. Decorate with a cherry.

❖ MINT JULEP ❖

2½ oz bourbon
1 tsp sugar
Soda
4 sprigs mint

In a highball glass, muddle eight to ten leaves of mint with sugar and a splash of soda. Fill the glass with shaved ice and pour on the bourbon. Garnish with a few sprigs of mint and serve with a straw. Arguments arise over whether the drink needs to be stirred or not. There is also some disagreement over whether to add orange, lemon, and/or cherry to the mint garnish. There is also a version that adds a few dashes of bitters to the glass before muddling. And for even more variety, top the finished drink with a few drops of brandy or rum. Like most classic drinks, each version has its devotees. Try them all. But not on the same night.

❖ OLD FASHIONED ❖

2 oz bourbon
1 tsp sugar
Dash of bitters
Splash of soda
Orange slice and cherry
Lemon twist

*In an old-fashioned glass (did you expect otherwise?), muddle the
sugar, the bitters, and a splash of soda. Some bartenders also
lightly muddle the slice of orange and the cherry. Add three ice
cubes and pour in the bourbon. Add a lemon twist, and if not
already muddled, garnish with the slice of orange and cherry.
Simple syrup may be used instead of sugar, the amount of either
adjusted for sweetness.*

❖OPENING❖
1½ oz bourbon or rye
½ oz grenadine
½ oz sweet vermouth
*Stir or shake all ingredients, and serve up in a cocktail glass or on
the rocks in an old-fashioned glass.*

❖ PRESBYTERIAN❖
Possibly the only drink named after a major religion. Could
there be others? A Catholic Cooler? A Buddhist Brandy? A
Lutheran Liqueur? A Jewish Julep?
2½ oz bourbon
2 oz ginger ale
2 oz soda
Lemon twist
*Stir the bourbon, ginger ale, and soda in a highball glass with
three ice cubes. Twist the lemon peel over the drink and drop it in.*

❖QUEBEC❖

1½ oz Canadian whiskey
½ oz dry vermouth
1½ tsp maraschino juice
1½ tsp Amer Picon
*Shake or stir with ice, and serve either up in a cocktail glass or on
the rocks in an old-fashioned glass. Either way you choose, try
rimming the glass with sugar.*

❖SAZERAC❖
3 oz bourbon
½ tsp sugar
5–6 drops Peychaud or angostura bitters
2–3 drops Pernod
Lemon twist
*Place the bourbon and sugar in an old-fashioned glass and stir.
Add one ice cube. Twist the lemon peel over the drink and drop it
in. Add the bitters and Pernod. Stir two or three times.*

Eat not to dullness, drink not to elevation.
—BEN FRANKLIN

❖ ❖ ❖ SEA COW ❖ ❖ ❖

The sea cow won a silver medal at the Sixteenth International Cocktail Competition in October 1982. It was created by Steve Herbert, the beverage manager at the Four Seasons Hotel in Toronto. Don't be deterred from mixing one just because you don't happen to have a Zwiesel crystal "Meran" white wine glass to serve it in. It's a winner even in an ordinary wine glass.

½ oz rye whiskey
¾ oz dark crème de cacao
½ oz anisette
1½ oz cream
Green crème de menthe
Sugar
Nutmeg
Shake ingredients with ice, and strain into a wine glass rimmed with sugar and green crème de menthe. Sprinkle the top with nutmeg.

❖ SOUL KISS COCKTAIL ❖

This sounds like something your parents told you never to try, but actually it's quite mellow and only dangerous if it leads on to frequent repetition!

1 oz bourbon
1 oz dry vermouth
½ oz Dubonnet
½ oz orange juice
Shake well with ice, and strain into a cocktail glass or over ice in an old-fashioned glass.

❖ TURKEY SHOOT ❖

Wild Turkey bourbon
Anisette
Fill a pony glass five-sixths up with Wild Turkey. Float anisette on top. Serve and drink as a shot.

❖ WARD 8 ❖

Here are the basic ingredients for a Daisy but there are some dramatic little flourishes that move it into a category all its own.

2 oz bourbon
Juice of ½ lemon
1 tsp sugar
½ oz grenadine
Dash of soda
Orange and lemon slices and cherry
Shake bourbon, lemon juice, sugar, grenadine with ice. Strain either into a cocktail glass or an old-fashioned glass with ice. Rinse out the shaker with the dash of soda and splash it into the drink. Garnish with fruit.

❖ WHISKEY EGGNOG ❖

2–3 oz bourbon or rye
1 tsp sugar
1 egg
Milk
Nutmeg

Shake all ingredients, except the milk, with ice and strain into a collins glass. Top with milk and sprinkle with nutmeg.

❖ WHISKEY SOUR ❖

Sours are simply liquors mixed with lemon juice and sugar, usually decorated with a slice of orange and a cherry. Here's the famous and popular Whiskey Sour, but substitute other liquors for variety.

2 oz bourbon
½ oz lemon juice
1 tsp sugar
Orange slice and cherry

Shake bourbon, lemon juice, and sugar with ice, and strain into a sour glass. Garnish with fruit.

❖ WHISKEY TODDY (COLD) ❖

Here are two recipes for the Whiskey Toddy, one hot, one cold. The hot toddy has been and always will be the perfect cold remedy.

2 oz bourbon or rye
½ tsp sugar
2 tsp water
Lemon twist

Dissolve sugar in water in an old-fashioned glass. And ice cubes and whiskey. Stir and garnish with a twist of lemon.

WHISKEY TODDY (HOT)

2 oz bourbon or rye
1 tsp sugar
Boiling water
Lemon slice
Nutmeg

Place sugar in an old-fashioned glass. Fill the glass two thirds with boiling water. Stir to dissolve sugar. Add the whiskey, stir, garnish with a slice of lemon. Sprinkle the top with nutmeg.

❖ WHISPERS OF THE FROST ❖
COCKTAIL

1 oz bourbon
1 oz sherry
1 oz port
1 tsp sugar
Lemon and orange slices

Shake with ice and strain into a cocktail glass. Garnish with slices of lemon and orange.

SCOTCH

In 1909 a Royal Commission, deciding matters related to "whiskey and other potable spirits," ruled that Scotch was a "whiskey made in Scotland." Of course, it's not called "Scotch" in Scotland. The Scots (who are erroneously called "the Scotch" in America) call it "whisky," not Scotch. And you'll probably not notice through a thick Scottish burr (not brogue; the Irish have a brogue, the Scots have a burr) that they elided the "e" in whiskey, pronouncing it just as they spell it—whisky. Now that that's cleared up, what is it—this whisk(e)y made in Scotland and called Scotch?

Scotch is indeed a whiskey, made from barley that has begun to sprout and is thus called "malted barley." Since grain sprouts in the springtime and Scotch distillers want to produce Scotch year round, they perform a neat trick they call "foolin' the barley" in which warm and wet springtime conditions are simulated so the unsuspecting grain will germinate and produce the enzyme, maltase, that will turn the fermenting grain into sugar. The grain is dried over peat fires which give Scotch its peaty, smoky flavor. Using waters from Scottish streams (which hold their own secrets!), the final spirit is aged in oak barrels for a minimum of three years. This malt Scotch is produced primarily in the Highlands where over a hundred distilleries, each producing its own brand, account for over a hundred different malt whiskeys.

And so much for the high road. The low road to Scotchland goes through the Lowlands and the Borders where less than fifteen distilleries produce over half the whiskey made in Scotland. This is blended Scotch, which consists of a combination of malt and other grain whiskeys, primarily corn and unmalted barley, which is not dried over peat fires. Blended Scotches are lighter and have a less smoky taste. There is no legal regulation determining the percentage of malt to grain whiskeys. Sometimes fifty different whiskeys will go into a blended Scotch, the type and proportion determining the aroma, color, and taste. The year on the label indicates the age of the youngest whiskey in the brew. Obviously, the more malt Scotch in a blend, the more it will taste "Scotchy." Most blended brands, however, are primarily grain rather than malt whiskey.

Since Scotch must come from Scotland, confusion arises over "bulk" Scotches and "bottled in Scotland" Scotches. The large batches sent to foreign countries in bulk are not bottled in Scotland. Notice the label. If it reads only "distilled and blended in Scotland," you have a bulk Scotch. The quality of bulk Scotches can vary from batch to batch, and it will probably be lighter and less expensive. For both reasons, many people prefer it for mixing in cocktails where the heavy Scotch taste is diluted and an expensive brand is not needed.

A label that reads "bottled in Scotland" really means it. About two thirds of the Scotch on the market is bottled in Scotland. It is generally older, consists of better blends, contains more malt whiskeys, and is of a better quality.

The history of Scotland's whiskey is much like America's whiskey. Both were first produced by farmers in remote areas and taxed against their will by the central government. They resisted violently, continued to make whiskey illegally (sometimes in the basement of the local "kirk," i.e., church), and sold it surreptitiously through moonshiners, who in Scotland were called "smugglers." No Royal Commission has decreed whether moonshine must, in fact, be made at night by the light of the moon. Royal Commissions have, however, decreed the fate of smugglers.

With so much confusion over names and types and the similarity between bourbon whiskey and Scotch whisky, are they really similar? A resounding "No," from any Scotch lover. Scotch is stronger in flavor and does not mix well with other ingredients. Consequently, there are fewer good cocktails based on Scotch since it is less adaptable. Most Scotch is consumed neat, on the rocks, or with a touch of water or soda.

And how do you know if you're getting a good Scotch or a bad Scotch? Not to worry. As the Scots themselves say, "There's whisky and there's guid whisky, but there's nae bad whisky." Agreed?

❖ABERDEEN ANGUS❖

2 oz Scotch
1 oz Drambuie
1 tbsp honey
Juice of 1 lime

In a mug or toddy glass, stir the Scotch, honey, and lime juice. Pour the Drambuie into a metal ladle and warm it over a low flame. Ignite the Drambuie and while it is burning, pour it into the mug. Stir and drink. It is advised to have someone who is not drinking these make succeeding ones for you!

❖AFFINITY❖

You might call this a "perfect" Rob Roy since it has all the ingredients for being one. Like the Perfect Manhattan it consists of the liquor base and both sweet and dry vermouth. The equal proportions, however, may cause some controversy and make some people disagree.

1 oz Scotch
1 oz dry vermouth
1 oz sweet vermouth
1 or 2 dashes of orange bitters

Shake all ingredients with ice and strain into a cocktail glass, or serve on the rocks in an old-fashioned glass.

❖BARBARY COAST❖

The Barbary Coast along Africa's north shore has always been a mixing spot for various cultures and peoples from all over. This drink is aptly named as it contains Scotch, rum, and gin in equal proportions.

¾ oz Scotch
¾ oz rum
¾ oz gin
¾ oz crème de cacao
¾ oz heavy cream

Shake all ingredients well with ice and strain into a cocktail glass. A variation of this drink omits the rum. When making it this way, increase the amount of each ingredient to one ounce.

❖BLOOD AND SAND❖

The name and the coloring of this drink conjurs up visions of soldiers spilling their blood on barbarous coasts, but the drink is a healthy juice concoction with a lot of life.

1 oz Scotch
1 oz cherry brandy
1 oz sweet vermouth
2 tbsp orange juice
Tonic (optional)

Shake with ice and strain into a cocktail glass, or serve on the rocks in an old-fashioned glass. Or serve in a highball glass and top with a splash of tonic water.

❖BLUE BLAZER❖

There are hot drinks, and there are hot drinks. Some are merely served warm. This one, however, is served with flames and all. I suggest you practice it before attempting to entertain your guests by preparing one in front of them. Once perfected, the show is all yours!

3 or 4 oz Scotch
1 tsp sugar or 1 tbsp honey
3 oz boiling water
Nutmeg
Lemon twist

Warm two metal mugs with handles. Dissolve the sugar or honey in one mug of boiling water. Warm the Scotch in a ladle over a low flame; then pour it quickly into the second mug. Ignite it. While it is still burning, pour the Scotch into the first mug, and then back and forth from mug to mug until the applause dies down or the stream of liquid fire gives out. Garnish with the lemon peel and powder the surface with nutmeg.

❖BOBBY BURNS❖

Named for the Scottish poet who always had a good word to say for the pleasures and camaraderie of imbibing spirits, this drink would make the poet in anyone wax mellowly about its fine ingredients.

1½ oz Scotch
1½ oz sweet vermouth
1½ tsp Bénédictine
Lemon twist

Stir with ice, and strain into a cocktail glass or over ice in an old-fashioned glass. Garnish with a lemon peel. A variation of the recipe calls for three-quarter ounce of sweet vermouth and three-quarter ounce of dry vermouth instead of just sweet vermouth.

❖CAMERON'S KICK COCKTAIL❖

1½ oz Scotch
1½ oz Irish whiskey
Juice of ½ lemon
2 dashes of orange bitters

Shake with ice. Strain into a cocktail glass or over rocks in an old-fashioned glass. For a slightly different taste, substitute one-half teaspoon of orgeat syrup for the bitters.

> *Oh, Moon of Alabama*
> *We now must say good-bye*
> *We've lost our good old mama*
> *And must have whiskey*
> *Oh, you know why!*
> —BERTOLT BRECHT

❖ FLYING SCOTCHMAN ❖

1½ oz Scotch
1½ oz sweet vermouth
½ tsp sugar
Dash of bitters

Stir with ice, and strain into a cocktail glass or over ice in an old-fashioned glass. You may also have heard of this one as the Flying Scotsman.

❖ GODFATHER ❖

Both Godfathers and Godmothers are made with the almond-flavored liqueur from Italy called amaretto, but with Scotch it is paternal, with vodka it grows motherly.

2 oz Scotch
1 oz amaretto

Stir with ice and strain into an old-fashioned glass over ice.

❖ MAMIE GILROY ❖

2 oz Scotch
Juice of ½ lime
Dash of bitters
Soda

Pour Scotch, lime juice, and bitters into a collins glass filled with ice cubes. Top with soda and stir.

❖ MIAMI BEACH COCKTAIL ❖

1 oz Scotch
1 oz dry vermouth
1 oz grapefruit juice

Shake all ingredients with ice and strain into a cocktail glass, or serve over ice in an old-fashioned glass. For a long drink, serve in a highball glass and top with grapefruit juice.

❖ PAISLEY MARTINI ❖

Not the same as a Rob Roy. This is a real Martini but with a faint whisper of Scotch.

1 tsp Scotch
2 oz gin
½ oz dry vermouth
Lemon twist

Stir with ice, and strain into a cocktail glass or over ice in an old-fashioned glass. Twist and drop in the lemon peel.

❖ PRINCE EDWARD ❖

A cocktail named after Prince Edward would have to include the delicious liqueur that is purported to descend from

> *There's no such thing as bad whiskey. Some*
> *whiskeys just happen to be better than others. But*
> *a man shouldn't fool with booze until he's fifty;*
> *then he's a damn fool if he doesn't.*
>
> WILLIAM FAULKNER

his own special recipe, Drambuie. The Prince Edward is something like a tall Rusty Nail with the addition of vermouth and soda.

1½ oz Scotch
¾ oz dry vermouth
½ oz Drambuie
Soda
Orange slice and cherry

Shake Scotch, vermouth, and Drambuie with ice. Strain into an old-fashioned glass and top with soda. Garnish with the orange slice and cherry.

❖ ROB ROY ❖

The famous and infamous hero of the MacGregor clan. Lover, outlaw, and adventurer, his name continues to inspire acts of derring-do—such as switching the famous Manhattan from a bourbon to a Scotch-based drink.

1½ oz Scotch
¾ oz sweet vermouth

Stir with ice, and serve either up in a cocktail glass or on the rocks in an old-fashioned glass.

❖ RUSTY NAIL ❖

A simple, syrupy drink for Scotch lovers made with two fine products from Scotland. An excellent after-dinner drink for people who want to "stay with Scotch" from the earlier cocktail hour.

1½ oz Scotch
½ oz Drambuie

Pour Scotch over rocks in an old-fashioned glass. Float the Drambuie on top. Do not stir.

❖ SCOTCH COOLER ❖

A cooler is simply a liquor drink poured long with ginger ale. But the Scotch Cooler has a refreshing twist: a subtle taste of crème de menthe.

2 oz Scotch
Several dashes of white crème de menthe
Ginger ale

Pour Scotch and crème de menthe in a highball glass and fill it with ice cubes. Top with ginger ale or other carbonated beverage. Stir and serve.

❖ SCOTCH MIST ❖

Mists make excellent after-dinner drinks and this one is a particularly pleasing libation for Scotch drinkers.

2 oz Scotch
Lemon twist

Fill an old-fashioned glass with crushed ice and cascade the Scotch over it. Twist the lemon peel to release the aroma and lay it on the ice. Serve with a short straw.

❖ SCOTCH SOLACE ❖

Every country has its favorite drink to comfort the woebegone, the abandoned, the unrequited love. This one from Scotland includes the always comforting milk and honey.

1½ oz Scotch
1 tsp honey
¾ oz triple sec
⅔ cup milk
1½ oz heavy cream
Grated orange peel (optional)

Pour Scotch, honey, and triple sec into a highball glass filled with ice. Stir vigorously until the honey has dissolved. Add milk and cream. Stir. Sprinkle the top with a grated orange peel.

❖ SCOTCH SOUR ❖

The Scotch Sour is a bit more tart than the traditional Whiskey Sour. You may want to increase the amount of sugar if the recipe below is not to your liking. Although sours are meant to be sour, they don't have to make you pucker!

2 oz Scotch
½ oz lemon juice
1 tsp sugar
Orange slice and cherry

Shake Scotch, lemon juice, and sugar with ice and strain into a sour glass. Garnish with an orange slice and a cherry. Also tasty served on the rocks in an old-fashioned glass.

❖ SCOTCH STINGER ❖

2 oz Scotch
1½ oz white crème de menthe
Shake with ice and strain into a cocktail glass, or serve over ice in
an old-fashioned glass.

❖ THE SHOOT ❖

1 oz Scotch
1 oz dry sherry
1 tsp orange juice
1 tsp lemon juice or lime juice
½ tsp sugar
Shake all of the ingredients with ice and strain into a cocktail
glass, or serve over ice in an old-fashioned glass.

❖ THISTLE COCKTAIL ❖

1½ oz Scotch
1½ oz sweet vermouth
2 dashes of bitters
Stir with ice, and serve in a cocktail glass up or over ice in an old-
fashioned glass.

> **Miniver Cheevy, born too late,**
> **Scratched his head and kept on thinking;**
> **Miniver coughed and called it fate,**
> **And kept on drinking.**
> —E. A. ROBINSON

❖ WALTERS ❖

This is basically the Shoot without sherry, and the amounts
are adjusted so you won't feel cheated.
1½ oz Scotch
1 tbsp orange juice
1 tbsp lemon juice
Shake and strain into a cocktail glass. Garnish with a slice of
orange if you are still worried about the missing sherry.

❖ WHIZ BANG ❖

1½ oz Scotch
¾ oz dry vermouth
1 tsp grenadine
1 tsp Pernod
2 dashes orange bitters
Stir with ice, and strain into a cocktail glass or over ice in an old-
fashioned glass.

GIN

In the sixteenth century Franciscus de Boe, a medical professor at the University of Leiden, distilled a spirit from juniper berries (for medicinal purposes, of course!) and to the delight and dismay of generations to come, the result was gin. British soldiers fighting in the Lowlands during the reign of William of Orange, himself a Dutchman, found that a swallow or two or more of the medicinal substance gave them what soldiers today might call a "battlefield high." They, however, called it "Dutch courage," and those who returned took it home with them to England. It continued to be sold only in apothecary shops supposedly for the purpose of purifying or cleansing the blood. Eventually it found a home of its own in "gin shops," an early term for what would evolve into "the pub."

Because it is a neutral spirit that is not aged, it was relatively easy and cheap to produce. Once produced, it is bottled and ready to be sold. It quickly became a drink the poor could afford, even when they were broke, which they usually were. Cheap gin gave rise to "gin lanes"—dirty, dank winding alleys that wended through the slummy sections of England's industrial towns. For many of the poor, who were transplanted from the rural countryside and small villages to work in the cities, gin became the only solace in an age just discovering the problems and evils of industrialized urban life. For mothers who worked in the dark, Satanic factories, the "gin rag" was a common form of day care for infants: A rag tied in a knot and soaked in gin was given to the infant to suck on, a pacifier that produced generations of lower-class alcoholics.

In 1736 the Gin Act was passed to limit the production of gin and to ban its sales in some cases altogether. But like the later experiment in the 1920s, it was not only unenforceable but gave rise to dangerous home brews (not called "bath tub gin" back then since most homes had no bath tub!). The physical and mental effects of the underground recipes were often more dangerous than the original problem. The law was soon repealed. In the latter part of the nineteenth century, London gin producers devised a recipe that was safe, predictable, and wonderfully popular, a gin not as heavily flavored with juniper berries as the competing Dutch brands. Known as "London Dry," or just dry gin, it became the basis for most modern gins brewed in the English-speaking world.

Today, gin is produced from the distillation of grain which is then redistilled with juniper berries and other ingredients, such as fruit, bark, roots, and seeds. Depending on the proportions and substances used, gin will vary in terms of its herbal, wood, or even flowery aroma. In principle, however, the ageless, colorless spirit is considered relatively tasteless. The Dutch gins are heavier and retain a strong flavor of juniper. Some of the better Dutch brands are sold in stone crocks, but the container itself has little to do with "getting crocked." The old juniper berry is still the culprit, which is also responsible for the term "gin" itself. Juniper in Dutch is *genever* and in French *genievre,* but the vowel shift is probably due less to the English way of pronouncing the Continental words than to the fact that several centuries ago when the English were discovering the Dutch spirit Tuscany was the major source of juniper berries. In Italian juniper is *ginepro.*

To many people who swear they are not gin drinkers, the liquor still retains a decidedly medicinal aroma and taste, encouraging the substitution of other clear spirits for gin in traditional gin cocktails. Vodka is the favorite substitute, followed more recently by tequila. It is not unusual—even in English cocktail lounges—to hear an order for a Vodka Martini and even a Tequila Martini (rechristened "Tequini" by tequila zealots). Much of this produces a shudder among Martini drinkers. At any rate, the number of gin drinks is legion. Should you not be a gin drinker, however, many of the following recipes might be kinder to your palate with vodka.

> *A night of good drinking*
> *Is worth a year's thinking.*
> —CHARLES COTTON

❖BEAUTY SPOT COCKTAIL❖

This is almost the same drink as The Bronx, although the name surely would not give it away. Perhaps that much maligned borough of New York City needs something like the Beauty Spot to perk up its image!

1½ oz gin
1 tbsp orange juice
½ oz sweet vermouth
½ oz dry vermouth
Dash grenadine

Shake all ingredients, except the grenadine, with ice. Dash the grenadine into an empty cocktail glass and strain the drink into it.

❖BEES KNEES❖

You don't need bee netting to make or enjoy this drink, but you do need a snappy line about a bee's knees. Personally I don't have one to offer you. I've never even seen a bee's knees. And I don't intend to.

1½ oz gin
Juice of ½ lemon
1 tbsp honey

Stir with ice vigorously until the honey is dissolved. Serve up in a cocktail glass.

❖BERMUDA BOUQUET❖

This drink and the following are relaxing vacation drinks that should call back memories of the island, the foliage, the fruit, and the pink sand. The Bouquet has a nice cluster of citric aromatizers. You may want to experiment with a colorful array of fruit garnishes.

1½ oz gin
1 oz apricot brandy
½ oz triple sec
1 oz lemon juice
½ oz orange juice
1 tsp sugar
1 tsp grenadine

Shake all ingredients with ice and strain into a highball glass filled with ice.

❖BERMUDA ROSE❖

This gin and apricot brandy drink is not the full bouquet of the preceding cocktail. It is simpler, less complicated, and pinker.

1½ oz gin
1 tsp apricot brandy
1 tsp grenadine
1 tbsp lime juice

Shake all ingredients with ice and strain over ice cubes in an old-fashioned glass.

❖BOSTON COCKTAIL❖

This drink does not vary considerably from a Bermuda Rose, which uses lime juice instead of lemon juice and a bit more grenadine.

1½ oz gin
1 oz apricot brandy
½ oz lemon juice
Dash of grenadine
Shake all ingredients with ice. Strain into a cocktail glass.

❖THE BRONX❖

If you can't bring yourself to offer your guests a drink called The Bronx either because you're from there or you can't shake the unfavorable image this New York borough has acquired in recent years, you'll find that the Beauty Spot Cocktail described earlier is practically the same drink.

1½ oz gin
½ oz dry vermouth
½ oz sweet vermouth
½ oz orange juice
Dash lemon juice
Orange slice
Shake with ice, and serve up in a cocktail glass or over the rocks in an old-fashioned glass. Decorate with orange slice.

❖CLOVER CLUB❖

There are several gin and lime drinks, but this one captures its own unique flavor and consistency with added egg white. For a creamy version of this drink, try a Pink Lady.

1½ oz gin
1 tsp grenadine
Juice of ½ lime
1 egg white
Shake ingredients together with ice until very cold and strain into a cocktail glass.

❖DEEP SEA COCKTAIL❖

If you enjoy this drink, try a Gloom Raiser. It's practically the same except for the grenadine which replaces the bitters. A Merry Widower is also very similar but has a few dashes of Bénédictine in it. In any case, I wouldn't don my scuba equipment after a few of these.

1½ oz gin
1½ oz dry vermouth
4 drops Pernod
2 dashes orange bitters
Olive and lemon twist
Stir with ice and strain into a cocktail glass. Twist a lemon peel over the drink and drop it in. Add the olive.

❖ FIFTY-FIFTY ❖

This drink is sometimes called a Gin and French. Half England, half France. A precarious drink. Any tampering with the proportions and you are dangerously flirting with the Martini.

1½–2 oz gin
1½–2 oz dry vermouth
Stir with ice. Serve up in a cocktail glass.

❖ FLORIDA ❖

½ oz gin
½ oz kirschwasser
½ oz triple sec
1¼ oz orange juice
1 tsp lemon juice
Shake with ice, and serve either up in a cocktail glass or over rocks in a highball glass.

❖ GIBSON ❖

The Gibson girls of magazine fame of course drank Martinis but very special ones. Pearl onions replaced the olives. And why not? Nothing but the most precious and exquisite for the paragons of feminine beauty.

Gin
Dry vermouth
2 pearl onions
See directions for Martinis (p. 57).

❖ GIN ALOHA ❖

1½ oz gin
1 tbsp triple sec
1 oz pineapple juice
Dash of bitters
Shake with ice. Serve up in a cocktail glass.

❖ GIN AND BITTERS ❖

This drink is simplicity itself. Some people refer to it as Pink Gin. It can also give you the pink eye if you drink too many of them. At that point, you may begin to eliminate the bitters (making it even simpler). The problem is you won't know that you're fogetting the bitters because it will continue to look pink.

Gin
Bitters
No specific amounts are necessary. That's the danger. Shake a few drop of bitters into a cocktail glass and roll them around until the inside of the glass is coated with bitters. Then add as much gin as you wish. No ice. Save it for the icepack tomorrow morning.

❖ GIN AND TONIC ❖

2 oz gin
Tonic
Lime wedge
Pour gin into a highball or collins glass filled with ice. Top with tonic and stir. Add the lime wedge.

❖ GIN BUCK ❖

1½ oz gin
1 oz lemon juice
Ginger ale
Pour all ingredients into an old-fashioned glass with ice. Stir. A highball or collins glass may be used for a taller drink with more ginger ale. Other spirits besides gin may be used. Don't pass the buck; experiment!

❖ GIN COOLER ❖

2–3 oz gin
½–1 oz lemon or lime juice
1 tsp sugar
Ginger ale
Lime, lemon, or orange slices
Shake gin, juice, and sugar with ice, and strain into a collins glass filled with fresh ice cubes. Top with ginger ale and garnish with a slice of your favorite citrus fruit.

❖ GIN DAISY ❖

2 oz gin
Juice of ½ lemon
½ tsp sugar
1 tsp raspberry syrup or grenadine
Soda
Orange slice, cherry, and raspberry
Shake with ice and strain into a small stem or sour glass. Add one cube of ice. Top with soda, and decorate with some combination of fruit.

❖ GIN FIZZ ❖

Fizzes are very much like Collinses. Basically they consist of a base liquor, lemon juice, sugar, and soda. But they are shorter, and if you prepare them correctly, they fizz. Regardless of the base liquor, there are specialty ingredients that turn fizzes into specialty fizzes. For instance, add the white of an egg and call it a Silver Fizz; the yolk transforms the drink into a Golden Fizz; the white of an egg and a sprig of mint create the Bootleg Fizz; two teaspoons of heavy cream produces the Cream Fizz; and a sprig of mint alone on top of the fizz is called an Alabama Fizz.

2 oz gin
1 oz lemon juice
1 tsp sugar
Soda

Shake gin, lemon juice, and sugar with ice. Strain into a highball glass and fill with soda, stirring simultaneously and zestily to make it fizz. No ice is needed, but one or two cubes spinning merrily in the drink adds to the sparkle.

❖ GIN GIMLET ❖

Gimlets are short drinks consisting of gin or vodka and lime juice. Of course, fresh lime juice may be used, but over the years drinkers have become accustomed to Rose's brand of lime juice, and now a gimlet made with anything else can taste like another drink altogether. Proportions differ among gimlet drinkers as to the amount of gin and lime juice. Experiment and discover your favorite combination. Vodka gimlets are perfect for people who do not like gin.

2 oz gin
1–2 oz Rose's lime juice (or juice of fresh lime)

Shake with ice, and strain into a cocktail glass or over ice in an old-fashioned glass.

❖ GIN SWIZZLE ❖

2 oz gin
Juice of 1 lime
1 tsp sugar
2 dashes of bitters
Soda

First, mix lime juice and sugar in a collins glass with about two ounces of soda. Fill the glass with ice. Add bitters, gin, and top with soda. Use a swizzle stick to stir.

❖ GLOOM RAISER ❖

There are other "gloomy" drinks that have nothing in common with the famous Gloom Raiser, to wit, Gloom Lifters and Gloom Chasers. See "Bourbon and Rye" for a Lifter and "Liqueurs" for a Chaser. The following drink, a Gloom Raiser, is very similar to another gin drink called a Deep Sea Cocktail, which uses bitters instead of grenadine.

2 oz gin
1½ oz dry vermouth
2 dashes of Pernod
Dash of grenadine

Stir with ice and strain into a cocktail glass.

❖ GOLDEN FIZZ ❖

This is the same drink as a Gin Fizz, but it gets its golden hue from the egg yolk.

1½ oz gin
1 oz lemon juice
½ tbsp sugar
1 egg yolk
Soda

Shake gin, sugar, lemon juice, and egg yolk thoroughly with ice. Strain into a highball glass and top with soda. Stir. No ice.

❖KNICKERBOCKER COCKTAIL❖

This drink is a variation on a Martini and should not be confused with the Knickerbocker Special which is a rum drink of exotic complexity.

1½ oz gin
¾ oz dry vermouth
¼ oz sweet vermouth
Lemon twist

Stir vermouth and gin with ice until chilled, and strain to serve up in a cocktail glass. Twist a lemon peel over it, rim the glass, and drop it in.

❖ LEAVE IT TO ME ❖

A very definite drink, not just left to the bartender's sense of whimsy. Nevertheless, check out the variation on this drink below. You might decide that it really should be left up to the bartender.

1 oz gin
½ oz dry vermouth
½ oz apricot brandy
½ tsp lemon juice
Dash grenadine

Shake with ice and strain into a cocktail glass. One variation is to substitute a teaspoon of raspberry liqueur and a half teaspoon of maraschino juice for the vermouth and apricot brandy. Increase the amount of gin about half an ounce or so. Grenadine optional.

❖MARTINI❖

The Martini is such a precious drink to its devotees, I hesitate to describe one. Martinis fall along a continuum of dry to *dry!!* and only the individual Martini drinker knows where along the scale his or her favorite can be found. No one agrees on the best or perfect Martini. Even when you have just consumed one, there seems to be a better one hovering just over the horizon. It is an endless quest, an ever-receding grail.

A regular Martini (pardon the expression!) is usually two parts gin to one part dry vermouth. From here you slowly move along the continuum through five to one all the way to eight to one. There is probably another zone beyond this one, but travelers there have not returned to tell us about it. Some people seeking the ultimate in dry Martinis merely whisper the word "vermouth" over the gin.

> *You can no more keep a martini in the refrigerator than you can keep a kiss there. The proper union of gin and vermouth is a great and sudden glory; it is one of the happiest marriages on earth and one of the shortest-lived.*
>
> —BERNARD DE VOTO

Controversy rages over whether a Martini should be shaken or stirred. Nondrinkers even argue over whether Martini drinkers can really tell the difference. Supposedly, shaking a Martini bruises the gin. Stirring is gentler. Martinis may be served up in cocktail glasses or over rocks in old-fashioned glasses. They are garnished with an olive (or two) or a lemon twist, or both. Whispering "olive" or "lemon" over the drink doesn't seem to have any noticeable effect.

Martinis made with vodka are called either Vodka Martinis or Vodkatinis. If you use tequila, it is called a Tequila Martini early in the evening and a Tequini later in the night. The latter is the newer and sometimes unavoidable name.

❖ MERRY WIDOW FIZZ ❖

Whether you "go off to Maxim's" for this drink or drink it in your own arbor, it's the same as a Gin Fizz with the addition of orange juice.

1½ oz gin
Juice of ½ orange
Juice of ½ lemon
1 tsp sugar
Soda

Shake gin, juices, and sugar with ice well, and strain into a highball glass with two ice cubes. Fill to the top with soda and stir. For a more frothy drink add an egg white to the first four ingredients and mix in a blender. Pour into a highball glass with ice. Then top with soda and stir.

❖ MERRY WIDOWER ❖

This may sound like a masculine version of the Merry Widow, a drink made with Dubonnet and dry vermouth, but as you can see, it isn't. In fact, it has more in common with a Gloom Raiser and Deep Sea Cocktail than with a Merry Widow.

1½ oz gin
1½ oz dry vermouth
2 dashes of Bénédictine
2 dashes of Pernod
Dash of bitters
Lemon twist

Stir the ingredients with ice and strain into a cocktail glass. Serve with a twist of lemon.

GIN

❖ NEGRONI ❖

2 oz gin
1 oz sweet vermouth
1 oz Campari
Splash of soda (optional)
Orange slice

Stir or shake with ice. Serve in a cocktail glass or over ice in an old-fashioned glass. Add a splash of soda and garnish with an orange slice. Some bartenders recommend equal parts of gin, vermouth, and Campari, omitting the soda.

❖ ORANGE BLOSSOM ❖

This fanciful drink is also known as the Adirondack and the Golden Gate, depending, I suppose, on which coast you live and drink.

2 oz gin
1½ oz orange juice
1 tsp sugar
Orange slice

Shake with ice and strain into a cocktail glass. For a tangier version, add one or two teaspoons of curaçao and two teaspoons of lemon or lime juice. Garnish with a slice of orange.

❖ PAISLEY MARTINI ❖

2 oz gin
½ oz dry vermouth
1 teaspoon Scotch
Lemon twist

Stir with ice, and strain into cocktail glass or over ice in an old-fashioned glass. Twist and drop in the lemon peel. If the proportions of gin and vermouth given here are not to your liking, change them to suit your taste, and adjust the Scotch accordingly.

❖ PARADISE ❖

Change the type of juice and brandy on this drink, add some sugar and soda, and you've got the classic Singapore Sling.

1½ oz gin
1 oz orange juice
½ oz apricot brandy
Orange slice

Shake gin, juice, and brandy with cracked ice, and strain into a cocktail glass. Garnish with a slice of orange.

❖ PINK LADY ❖

Some men and a few liberated women won't order this drink by name. If you're looking for a reasonable facsimile, check out the Clover Club.

1½ oz gin
1 tsp grenadine
½ oz heavy cream
1 egg white
Shake all ingredients with ice until cold, and strain into a cocktail glass or a champagne glass.

❖ RAMOS FIZZ ❖

The Ramos Fizz is a fizz to end all fizzes. The egg white and the heavy cream play special tricks in this drink. The drink was created by and named after Henry C. Ramos, who went to New Orleans in 1888 and ran a drinking establishment on the site now occupied by the Fairmont Hotel.

2 oz gin
¼ cup heavy cream
1 egg white
Juice ½ lemon
1 tbsp sugar
1 tsp orange-flower water
Soda
Shake all ingredients, except the soda, with cracked ice. Shake well. Strain into a highball glass and fill with soda. One or two ice cubes won't hurt. Stir.

❖ SALTY DOG ❖

You *can* teach an old dog new tricks. There is a variation on this old favorite that should cause it to be renamed something like "Sweet Poochken." See below.

1½ oz gin
5–6 oz grapefruit juice
Pinch of salt
Pour gin and juice over ice in a highball glass and stir. Add a pinch of salt and serve. New trick: substitute vodka for gin and (yes, you knew it was coming!) a pinch of sugar instead of salt.

❖ SINGAPORE SLING ❖

This classic gin drink has no equal according to those who love it. But many people admit that half the mystique is in the name. Romance. Mystery. Intrigue. Try a Paradise Cocktail too. The name is just as exotic, and the basic ingredients are similar.

2 oz gin
1 oz cherry brandy
1 oz lemon juice
1 tsp sugar
Soda
Cherry, orange, or lemon slice
Shake gin, lemon juice, and sugar with ice, and strain into a collins glass filled with ice. Fill to within a half inch of the top with soda. Float the cherry brandy on top and garnish with a selection of fruit suggested above.

❖ SNICKER ❖

2 oz gin
1 oz dry vermouth
½ tsp maraschino
1 tsp sugar
1 egg white
Dash of orange bitters
Shake all ingredients with ice and strain over ice in
a highball glass.

❖ SOUTHERN BRIDE ❖

This drink is a sweet, pleasant diversion for people who enjoy gin and grapefruit juice, usually mixed as a Salty Dog. Served in a champagne glass and with a dash of maraschino juice, this drink warrants the more elegant name.

2 oz gin
1 oz grapefruit juice
½ tsp maraschino juice
Shake with ice, and serve up in a cocktail glass or a champagne
glass.

❖ TOM COLLINS ❖

The family of Collins stretches through the bars and saloons of many lands. The paterfamilias is said to have been a London barman named John Collins who laid whiskey down in the late nineteenth century. His offspring are legion. Tom is a gin drink, John Collins is now made with bourbon, Mike Collins is made with Irish whiskey, Pedro is a rum drink, and a Pierre Collins is a cognac concoction. I'm sure an Ivan Collins and a Carlos Collins already have their feet on the brass rail and are ordering a Vodka Collins and a Tequila Collins respectively. If you can't sire your own Collins, try adopting one of the above.

2–3 oz gin
½–1 oz lemon juice
1 tsp sugar
Soda
Cherry, lemon slice, and orange slice
Shake gin, sugar, and lemon juice with ice. Strain into a collins
glass (naturally!), add several ice cubes, and fill with soda.
Garnish with a cherry and fruit slices. Drink with a straw.

❖ YALE COCKTAIL ❖

Yes, Virginia, there is a Harvard Cocktail. See "Brandy."

1½ oz gin
½ oz dry vermouth
1 tsp blue curaçao (or more)
Dash of bitters
Stir all ingredients with slow conservative revolutions. Then serve
up in a cocktail glass.

VODKA

From the plains of northeastern Europe comes a drink steeped in controversy—vodka. Etymologists squabble over its Slavic roots. Is it the Russian word for "little water" (*voda* meaning water)? Or is it the Polish word for "little water" (*woda* meaning water)? It is agreed that the *k* is a diminutive. Like the shifting borderland between these two nations, the drink itself has origins that will probably never be drawn with any certainty or finality. The headquarters for Smirnoff is located in Lvov, a city that has been Polish more often than Russian, even though today it is inside the Soviet Union. Vodka is reputed to have been concocted originally from potato mash somewhere in the wintry region of northeastern Europe to provide a neutral spirit that would not freeze at 32 degrees Fahrenheit as does water. Not only was it a thirst quencher that could withstand the blasting winds of subfreezing temperatures, but a quick stiff shot could warm the coldest gut in a land where winter comes early and stays long.

In the West, vodka is a relative newcomer to the world of popular drinking habits. Until a generation ago, it was thought to be a volatile drink consumed only in quaint backward villages of Eastern Europe where anarchists, terrorists, and other political undesirables gulped it neat, braced themselves grimly on wooden tables awaiting its ruthless wallop, and got what they deserved. But in the late 1930s a southern entrepreneur imported Smirnoff and advertised it as "White Whiskey. No taste. No smell." A come-on that excited a generation of drinkers who had suffered through the Prohibition Era of speakeasies and federal agents sniffing out illegal drinking establishments. Vodka seemed to be the answer to the old-time morality that rued the day Prohibition was repealed—a godsend to the counties that continued to drink wet and vote dry after 1933. But World War II interrupted the importation of "white whiskey," and it wasn't until Smirnoff launched a successful advertising campaign in the 1950s that vodka really caught on with Western drinkers, an ironic fact considering Communist Russia launched a satellite, and many people in the West feared the Cold War had moved into outer space.

Today, vodka is produced from a variety of substances, not just potatoes, including grapes and beets. In the United States most vodka is from the distillation of corn and wheat. Being a neutral, colorless, and almost tasteless liquor, the base fermentation is undetectable. No aging is needed. Some brands do, however, add flavoring agents. Zubrowka inserts a blade of buffalo grass that grows on the wide plains of Poland. If you experiment with various brands, you'll notice there is a subtle but distinct flavor to many of them.

But vodka is relatively unobtrusive and thus provides a strong base liquor that will not unfairly dilute the flavor of many mixed drinks, be they made with orange juice, tomato juice, Kahlúa, or just plain tonic water and fresh lime. The number of vodka cocktails has proliferated in the last thirty years or so, considering it was formerly a spirit limited to a little known, little visited, and little understood section of the world.

❖ APRÈS SKI ❖

2 oz vodka
1½ oz green crème de menthe
1½ oz Pernod
Lemonade
Lemon slice
Sprig of mint
Shake vodka, crème de menthe, and Pernod with ice, and strain into a highball glass with several cubes of ice. Top with lemonade, garnish with lemon and mint, and serve with two long straws.

❖ ATLANTIC AVENUE ❖

This drink was created for the Atlantic Antic, a twelve-block street fair held on Brooklyn's famous avenue from Flatbush to the New York harbor. It may remind you of a more exotic variation of the Salty Dog of which Atlantic Avenue has its own fair share.

1½ oz vodka
1½ oz grapefruit juice
½ oz sweet vermouth
Tonic
Cherry
Shake vodka, grapefruit juice, and vermouth with ice. Strain into a highball glass with ice. Top with tonic. Garnish with a cherry.

❖❖❖ THE BARRISTERS ❖❖❖ SPECIAL

Just across the street from Ontario's classic old law school Osgoode Hall is the Barristers' Bar located in the Hotel Toronto, a well-known rendezvous for business people and a natural haunt of lawyers and judges. If you ordered a Barristers Special and drank it relaxed in the burgundy brown and deep orange leather chairs surrounded by book-lined walls, you'd receive a barrister's headstick made from a very expensive mold of an old English judge as a souvenir, hand-painted and baked to perfection.

1 oz vodka
1 oz white rum
½ oz rock candy syrup
½ oz pineapple juice
½ oz lemon juice
Pineapple chunk and cherry
Blend all ingredients with a scoop of crushed ice and serve in a collins glass. Garnish with fruit.

❖ BEER BUSTER ❖

1½ oz vodka
Beer
2 dashes of Tabasco sauce
Pour vodka into a beer stein or a highball glass. Top with beer and add Tabasco sauce. Stir and serve.

❖ BLACK MAGIC ❖

2 oz vodka
1 oz coffee liqueur
1 dash of lemon juice
Lemon twist
Stir all ingredients with ice. Strain into an old-fashioned glass filled with ice. Garnish with a lemon twist.

❖ BLACK RUSSIAN ❖

2 oz vodka
1 oz Kahlúa or any coffee-flavored brandy
Shake with ice and strain into a cocktail glass. When ordered on the rocks, some bartenders pour the vodka over the ice and trickle the dark colored Kahlúa or other coffee-flavored brandy over the top and serve without stirring.

❖❖❖ BLOODY CAESAR ❖❖❖

This drink was invented in the Canadian Rockies and moved back east to the Westin Hotel Toronto with its inventor Walter Chell. It seems guests in Toronto love it as much as those who first sipped it in Calgary, Alberta, fifteen years ago. Like most "bloody" drinks it's a variation on the Bloody Mary.

1½ oz vodka
5 oz tomato juice
2 dashes of Worcestershire sauce
Celery salt and pepper to taste
½ lime
Celery stalk

In a tall highball glass half filled with ice, add salt, pepper, and Worcestershire sauce. Pour in vodka and tomato juice. Squeeze half a lime and drop in the shell. Stir and garnish with the celery.

❖ BLOODY MARY ❖

George Jessel claims to have thought this drink up. But then so do others, including a couple of New York bartenders. Whatever its origin, it has become one of the most popular morning-after pick-me-ups. If you are serving it at a morning brunch, try pouring the vodka and tomato juice into their glasses and serving the other ingredients on a tray so each guest can spice up the drink as he or she desires.

1½ oz vodka
3 oz tomato juice
½ oz lemon juice
½ tsp Worcestershire sauce
2–3 drops of Tabasco sauce
Celery salt and pepper to taste
Lime or lemon wedge
Celery stalk

Shake well with ice and strain into a highball glass with ice. Garnish with one or more of the garnish items.

❖ BLUE MONDAY ❖

1½ oz vodka
1 oz triple sec
½ oz blue curaçao

Stir with ice. Strain into a cocktail glass or over ice in an old-fashioned glass.

❖ BULLSHOT ❖

This drink is similar to the Bloody Mary in that the spicy ingredients can be added in varying proportions depending on individual taste. So everyone is happy, just fill their glasses with vodka and bouillon, and serve the other ingredients on a tray so each guest can doctor up the basics as each sees fit.

2 oz vodka
4 oz beef bouillon
½ tsp Worcestershire sauce
Dash of Tabasco sauce or cayenne pepper
Salt
Juice of ½ lemon
Lemon slice

Shake well with ice. Serve in an old-fashioned glass with one ice cube. Garnish with a lemon slice.

❖ CAPE CODDER ❖

2 oz vodka
4 oz cranberry juice
Juice of ½ lime
Lime wedge

Shake ingredients with ice and strain into a collins glass filled with ice. Garnish with a lime wedge.

❖ CASABLANCA ❖

1½ oz vodka
½ oz advokaat
½ oz Galliano
Juice of 1 lemon
1 tbsp orange juice
Orange slice

Shake with ice, and strain into a champagne glass or a cocktail glass with crushed ice. Garnish with an orange slice.

❖ CLAMATO COCKTAIL ❖

This drink is something like a Bloody Mary for the seafood lover. You might try experimenting with the other Bloody Mary ingredients to spice up the simple recipe given below.

2 oz vodka
1 oz Clamato or clam juice
3 oz tomato juice
Dash of Tabasco sauce

Shake all ingredients with ice and strain into an old-fashioned glass with ice.

❖ CREAMY SCREWDRIVER ❖

The Creamy Screwdriver is almost a complete breakfast. People who swear by eggs in the morning to rid themselves of hangovers may enjoy this morning drink since it contains the proverbial "hair of the dog" as well as the egg.

2–3 oz vodka
1 egg yolk
6 oz orange juice
2 tsp sugar

Mix all ingredients in a blender with crushed ice. Serve in a collins glass with ice.

❖ THE FLYING GRASSHOPPER ❖

With slightly altered proportions of the crème de menthe and crème de cacao, this drink becomes a Vodka Grasshopper.

1 oz vodka
¾ oz green crème de menthe
¾ oz white crème de cacao

Stir with ice. Serve up in a cocktail glass.

❖ GODMOTHER ❖

The matriarchal drink made with vodka instead of Scotch.
See Godfather under Scotch drinks.

1½ oz vodka
¾ oz amaretto
Pour ingredients in the above order over ice into an old-fashioned
glass. Stir once.

❖ GRAPE VODKA FROTH ❖

2 oz vodka
1 oz grape juice
1 oz lemon juice
1 egg white
Shake with ice or mix in a blender. Strain into a cocktail glass or
serve over ice in an old-fashioned glass.

❖ GREEN DRAGON ❖

This is the same as a White Spider only with green crème de
menthe instead of white. You may wonder why it was not
called a Green Spider. Try offering a green spider to your
guests and you'll see why.

2 oz vodka
1 oz green crème de menthe
Stir with ice and strain into a cocktail glass.

❖ HARRY WALLBANGER ❖

A more sophisticated cousin (or is it brother!?) to Harvey.

1½ oz vodka
1 oz Cointreau
2–3 oz orange juice
Champagne
Shake vodka, Cointreau, and orange juice with ice. Strain over ice
into a collins glass. Top with champagne.

❖ HARVEY WALLBANGER ❖

The story goes that Harvey was a surfer who bounced into
California bars after a hard day's work on the waves and
consoled himself with screwdrivers to which he added Galliano. One day he imbibed too many and "surfed" from one
wall to the other as he staggered out. From then on he was
known as "wall banger." So was the drink.

2 oz vodka
2 tbsp Galliano
6 oz orange juice
Shake vodka and orange juice with ice, and strain over ice in a
collins glass. Float Galliano on top.

❖ HEADLESS HORSEMAN ❖

2 oz vodka
Several dashes of bitters
Ginger ale
Orange slice

Pour vodka and bitters into a collins glass. Add a few ice cubes. Top with ginger ale and stir. Garnish with the orange.

❖ HONG KONG FIZZ ❖

Legend has it that this drink was concocted by Maude Jones, a famous brothel keeper in Hong Kong in the nineteenth century. She could down almost a dozen of these every day before lunch. She probably had to. There was no stopping her.

1 oz vodka
1 oz gin
½ oz yellow Chartreuse
½ oz green Chartreuse
½ oz Bénédictine
½ oz lemon juice
Soda
Orange, lemon, and lime slices
Cherry

Shake everything, except the soda, with ice. Strain into a highball glass. Top with soda and garnish with the fruit.

❖ KAMAKAZEE ❖

1½ oz vodka
½ oz Rose's lime juice
½ oz triple sec
½ oz lemon juice
1 tsp sugar

Shake ingredients with ice and strain over ice in an old-fashioned glass.

❖ KANGAROO ❖

Don't let the name from "down under" fool you. A Vodka Martini by any other name would still be a ... well, a "Vodkatini."

2 oz vodka
¾ oz dry vermouth
Lemon twist

Stir vodka and vermouth with ice. Strain into a cocktail glass or over the rocks into an old-fashioned glass. Twist a lemon peel over the drink and drop it in.

❖ MOSCOW MULE ❖

The Russians did not invent this one. The Americans did. So the race is on!

2–3 oz vodka
2 tbsp lime juice
Ginger beer or ginger ale
Lime wedge

In a mug or beer stein pour the vodka and lime juice. Stir. Drop in two or three ice cubes. Fill with ginger beer. Stir again and garnish with a lime wedge.

❖ NUTTY RUSSIAN ❖

Nocello is the favorite liqueur for this cocktail, but other walnut-flavored liqueurs will work.

2 oz vodka
1 oz Nocello or any walnut-flavored liqueur

Shake with ice and strain over rocks in an old-fashioned glass.

❖ ROAD RUNNER ❖

1½ oz vodka
¾ oz amaretto
¾ oz coconut juice or coconut cream
Sugar
Nutmeg

Shake vodka, amaretto, and coconut juice with ice. Strain into a champagne glass rimmed with sugar. Sprinkle nutmeg on top.

❖ RUSSIAN BEAR ❖

With all these white and clear ingredients, the Russian Bear should resemble a polar bear.

1½ oz vodka
¾ oz white crème de cacao
1 tbsp heavy cream

Shake well with ice. Serve up in a cocktail glass.

❖ SCREWDRIVER ❖

Most people serve Screwdrivers in tall glasses filled with ice and orange juice. That's fine for hot days when you want to gulp down a zesty thirst quencher. But as a cocktail before dinner or brunch, serve the Screwdriver in an old-fashioned glass with ice and roughly equal parts of vodka and orange juice. Or serve chilled vodka and ice-cold juice in a cocktail glass with no ice.

2 oz vodka
Orange juice

Pour vodka over rocks in a highball glass and top with orange juice. Stir with a screwdriver (optional).

❖❖❖ SIR JOHN'S FOLLY ❖❖❖

This specialty drink was created for a baby shower at the Fox and Hounds Pub at the Cheshire Lodge in St. Louis. They tell us it went on to become "popular with young drinkers because of its color and flavor." Whatever the legal drinking age is, we presume it's not a drink for teetotalin' toddlers!

½ oz vodka
½ oz rum
1 oz sweet sour mix
2 oz orange juice
¼ oz blue curaçao
Orange slice

Blend all ingredients in a mixer. Serve in a snifter with crushed ice. Garnish with an orange slice.

❖❖❖ SOUTHAMPTON ❖❖❖ STINGER

At the Fox and Hounds Pub at the Cheshire Lodge in St. Louis, this drink is called a "Stinger" even though it's not made with white crème de menthe as are most Stingers. According to the folks at the Fox and Hounds, the origins of this specialty drink are "lost in history."

1 oz vodka
½ oz Galliano
½ oz apricot brandy

Mix ingredients in a blender and serve over rocks in a brandy snifter.

❖ SOVIET ❖

2 oz vodka
½ oz dry sherry
½ oz dry vermouth
Lemon twist

Shake with ice. Serve in an old-fashioned glass with ice. Garnish with a lemon twist.

❖ VODKA COLLINS ❖

Same as the Gin Collins; affectionately called the Tom Collins, only with vodka instead.

2 oz vodka
Juice of ½ lemon
1 tsp sugar
Soda
Slices of lemon and orange
Cherry

Shake vodka, lemon juice, and sugar with ice. Strain into a collins glass. Add three or four ice cubes and top with soda. Stir and garnish with fruit. Serve with a long straw.

❖ VODKA GIMLET ❖

Americans are the culprits. Gimlets were originated in the Orient by the British who, of course, preferred gin with Rose's lime juice. But as with other traditional British drinks, the New World enjoys substituting that other Old World spirit, vodka.

1½ oz vodka
½ oz Rose's lime juice
Lime wedge

Shake vodka and lime juice with ice, and strain into a cocktail glass or over ice in an old-fashioned glass. Squeeze the lime and drop it in.

❖VODKA SALTY DOG❖

The original Salty Dog was made with gin, but the vodka variation has become a favorite in many communities where, as they say, a salty dog will lick up most anything.

2 oz vodka
5 oz grapefruit juice
¼ tsp salt

Stir all ingredients with ice and strain into a highball glass filled with ice. As in the original Salty Dog recipe, sugar (as strange as it may sound) may be substituted for salt.

❖VODKA TONIC❖

2 oz vodka
Tonic
Lime slice or wedge

Pour vodka over ice in a highball glass. Fill with tonic water and stir. Garnish with fresh lime.

❖WATERMELON❖

Some people claim this actually tastes like watermelon. Others say it tastes like strawberry, orange, and lemon. Tastes vary.

1½ oz vodka
1 oz strawberry liqueur
1½ oz orange juice
Juice of ½ lemon
½ tsp sugar

Shake well with ice and strain over ice in an old-fashioned glass.

❖WHITE RUSSIAN❖

This variation on the Black Russian is perfect as a late night drink. The cream or milk helps to induce sleep and lines the stomach so that the stimulant spirits don't enter the bloodstream too quickly.

2 oz vodka
1 oz Kahlúa or any coffee-flavored brandy
2 tsp heavy cream

Shake with ice and serve in an old-fashioned glass. Some bartenders make the drink as they would a Black Russian and then pour the cream on the top and serve without stirring.

RUM

On his second voyage to the New World, Christopher Columbus brought sugarcane from the Canary Islands and thus began the colorful tradition that today is part of the economic and social life of every major Caribbean island—the production and consumption of rum. Rum! The very name conjures up epic fantasies of pirates, the British navy, the clash of sea battles, the infamous slave trade, the colonization of tropical lands by almost every nation of Western Europe. Perhaps no other spirit has had such a tempestuous history, as romantic, exotic, and mercurial as the tropical paradise from which it hails. The name and its derivations have origins lost in the rise and fall of empires and fierce tropical storms. Some authorities trace it to early forms of the English word "rumpus"—"rumbustion," "rumscallion"—suggesting the fracas and melee of pirate attacks or the drunken shore leave of British sailors. Others suggest it derives from "sacchrum," the Latin word for sugar.

In any event, rum has always been a popular, if infamous, drink. Beginning in the 1600s, the Triangular Trade brought molasses from the Caribbean to New England distilleries where it was processed into rum to be traded on the African coast for slaves who in turn were sold to work the sugar plantations of the West Indies. This scandalous and shameful era in the Western economy nevertheless served to introduce rum to many nations, and made it the prestige drink among upper-class Americans.

Indeed, the famous Whiskey Rebellion in our early history was not, in fact, a "rum rebellion" because the elite political leadership residing primarily on the east coast did not tax their darling rum, only whiskey, a cruder, less civilized drink enjoyed in the poorer backwoods territories. And in other nations, and at other times as well, because it is steeped in the mottled history and romance of faraway islands, rum has always held a special place of honor in the well-stocked bar.

Rum is made by distilling either the fermented juice from sugarcane or the molasses left once the sugar is removed. It is aged in barrels two to three years. Some rums, aged fifteen years or more, will be rich and smooth enough to be taken neat, like a fine brandy. By color rum is either white, amber (gold), or very dark. The white and amber rums are also light-bodied and have less molasses taste. They are drier, and, because they are thinner in flavor than the dark rum, behave much like vodka. They make excellent mixers in drinks that require a sound fruit juice flavor undisturbed by the spirit base. In fact, light rum is second to vodka in popularity because it is so adaptable.

The dark, heavy-bodied rum is fermented slower so molasses will develop, thus giving it a richer aroma and a tangier molasses flavor. The actual color, however, is as much caramel as molasses or the color from the barrel. A Jamaican rum is extra rich and syrupy due to its double distillation process and the use of "dunder," a residue from earlier distillations which, like sour mash in bourbon, brews a distinctively forceful spirit. To call someone a "dunderhead" implies the "dummy" is actually more of a "rummy" for over-indulging in the heady brew.

In recent days, lighter rum has truly invaded the marketplace, establishing its own territorial rights as it colonizes more and more shelf space in liquor stores. Because it mixes so unobtrusively with fruit and juice beverages, rum has become one of the favorite spiritous ingredients for specialty drinks, and there is hardly a bartender who has not felt the urge to experiment with rum to concoct a novelty drink. The festive, holiday character of many rum drinks, frequently served in pineapples, coconuts, tall frosted glasses, sometimes frozen and electrically colorful, and garnished with bouquets of berries, fruit pieces, even flowers, has inspired the proliferation of rum-based drinks. And why not? To sip a Piña Colada, Zombie, Daiquiri, Planter's Punch, or a humble Rum and Coke—even if not upgraded to a bona fide Cuba Libre—is to taste if only in fantasy, that exotic corner of the world—the West Indies.

One can drink too much, but one never drinks enough.
—GOTTHOLD EPHRAIM LESSING

❖ ACAPULCO ❖

There is another Acapulco made with tequila and pineapple. See Acapulco under tequila drinks.

1½ oz rum
¾ oz triple sec
1 tbsp lime juice
1 tsp sugar
½ egg white
Sprig of mint

Shake all ingredients with ice and strain over ice cubes in an old-fashioned glass. Garnish with a sprig of fresh mint.

❖ BACARDI COCKTAIL ❖

In some parts of the English-speaking world, all rum is called Bacardi as if that were the only type around This drink and the following, the Bacardi Special, must be made with the Bacardi brand if you are going to call them by it.

1½ oz Bacardi rum
1 oz lime juice
½ tsp grenadine

Shake with ice and serve in a cocktail glass.

❖ BACARDI SPECIAL ❖

The Bacardi Special is an interesting variation on the Bacardi Cocktail by the addition of gin and sugar. You must use Bacardi brand rum, however, if you plan to call it by the Bacardi name.

2 oz Bacardi rum
¾ oz gin
1 oz lime juice
Dash grenadine
½ tsp sugar

Hold the rum aside, and shake all the other ingredients with ice. Then, add the rum and shake again. Strain into a cocktail glass or a champagne glass.

❖❖❖ BANANA SMASH ❖❖❖

The Banana Smash is an original drink from the Hyatt Regency Waikiki in Honolulu. They suggest it be served in a zombie glass and garnished with an orchid. But landlocked bartenders on the mainland may have to settle for a less exotic display.

1 oz rum
½ oz vanilla extract
1 ripe banana
2 oz Half-and-Half
½ banana
Orchid

Blend first four ingredients in a mixer. Serve in a sixteen-ounce zombie glass and decorate with half a banana and an orchid.

❖ BATIDO DE PIÑA ❖

3 oz rum
⅔ cup coarsely chopped fresh pineapple
½–1 tsp sugar
Fresh mint
Blend the rum, pineapple, and sugar at high speed until smooth. Pour into a goblet half filled with crushed ice. Decorate with a sprig of fresh mint.

❖ BEACHCOMBER ❖

1½ oz rum
½ oz lime juice
½ oz triple sec or Cointreau
½ tsp maraschino juice
Sugar
Shake all ingredients except sugar with ice and strain into an old-fashioned glass rimmed with lime juice and sugar. Drop in one or two ice cubes.

❖ BLUE HAWAIIAN ❖

The Blue Hawaiian is a fun drink to experiment with. Keep the rum and blue curaçao but test out different types of juices and creams. Be careful though or the ethereal blue coloring may begin to slide into green or brown!

2 oz rum
½ oz blue curaçao
½ oz triple sec
1 oz pineapple juice
1½ oz coconut cream or plain heavy cream
Shake with ice. Strain into a cocktail glass, or serve over rocks in an old-fashioned glass.

❖ CHERRY RUM ❖

Although this is a cocktail, there's no reason why it can't be served as an after-dinner drink. Increase the amount of cherry brandy and cream and you'll have a rich dessertlike drink.

1½ oz rum
1½ tsp cherry-flavored brandy
1 tbsp heavy cream or more
Shake well with ice, and strain into a cocktail or champagne glass.

❖ CHINESE COCKTAIL ❖

1½ oz rum
½ oz triple sec
1 tablespoon grenadine
Dash of maraschino juice
Dash bitters
Shake with ice and serve up in a cocktail glass.

❖ CUBA LIBRE ❖

This is *not* a Rum and Coke. No directions are needed for a Rum and Coke. Nevertheless, many bartenders don't know the difference. Some of them try to get by the easy way by asking you if you'd like a wedge of lime with your Rum and Coke. If you say yes, you'll probably get the lazy bartender's Rum and Coke.

2 oz rum
1 lime
Coke

Squeeze the lime into a collins glass; muddle the lime rinds into a fruity pulp. Add four ice cubes and the rum. Top with Coke and stir. See the difference!

❖ DAIQUIRI ❖

Teddy Roosevelt had a "bully good time" in Cuba during the Spanish–American War. So did American engineers who stayed on afterward to bring the Cubans the benefits of American technology and, in exchange, discovered the Daiquiri. Invented by the crafty Yankee engineers, the Daiquiri was originally a long drink served in tall glasses. Later it was scaled down to become the shorter drink for the stemmed cocktail glass as we know it today.

2 oz rum
Juice 1 lime
1 tsp sugar
Dash of maraschino

Shake all ingredients with ice and strain into a cocktail glass.

FROZEN DAIQUIRI

A Frozen Daiquiri is only frozen for the first several minutes of its brief life. Scientifically minded devotees of this drink have attempted to discover the Frozen Daiquiri's half-life but the statistics when remembered are somewhat muddled. Some bartenders swear that the Frozen Daiquiri should be made with a tablespoon of triple sec. Some people swear that every Daiquiri should have triple sec. There are several varieties of Frozen Fruit Daiquiris. In general they are made according to the standard Frozen Daiquiri recipe but include the fruit or berry of your choice: Banana, strawberry, and cherry are the most popular. Add to the ingredients an ounce of fresh or frozen fruit and about an ounce (or more) of the fruit flavored liqueur, e.g., strawberry or a banana-flavored liqueur.

Mix all ingredients in a blender with ice until ice slush forms. Then pour into a cocktail glass and drink with a short straw.

❖❖❖ DORCHESTER ROYAL ❖❖❖

The Dorchester Royal was specially concocted to honor the royal wedding of Prince Charles and Princess Diana in July 1981. It continues to be a regal favorite at the Dorchester Hotel in London where it was first served.

1½ oz white rum
Dash of peach liqueur
Dash of pineapple juice
Dash of heavy cream
Dash of blue curaçao
Pineapple leaves and green cherry
Mix all ingredients with ice in a shaker. Strain into a tall champagne glass and serve straight up. Garnish with pineapple leaves and a green cherry.

❖ EL PRESIDENTE ❖

1½ oz rum
½ oz curaçao
½ oz dry vermouth
Couple dashes of grenadine
Dash of bitters (optional)
Stir with ice and strain into a cocktail glass. A variation on this recipe substitutes a half ounce of sweet vermouth for the curaçao and garnishes with an orange slice.

❖ FERNANDO ❖

This drink was invented on Cape Cod in 1983 by beach-combers who were tired of drinking Cape Codders.

1½ oz rum
Cranberry juice
Tonic
In a highball glass filled with ice, pour the rum and cranberry juice until approximately three fourths filled. Top with tonic and stir.

❖ FIREMAN'S SOUR ❖

2 oz rum
½ oz grenadine
Juice of 1 lime
½ tsp sugar
Soda or tonic
Lemon slice and cherry
Shake rum, grenadine, lime juice, and sugar with ice, and strain into an old-fashioned glass or a highball glass with ice. Top with soda or tonic. Garnish with a lemon slice and cherry.

❖ GROG ❖

2 oz rum
1 tbsp lemon juice
1 tsp sugar
3 or 4 cloves
1 cinnamon stick (or ground cinnamon to taste)
Boiling water
Lemon slice
In a heat-proof mug, mix all the ingredients with boiling water until the sugar has dissolved. Garnish with a lemon slice.

❖❖❖ HARPOON ❖❖❖

From the windswept Moors Restaurant in Provincetown, Cape Cod, comes this original drink flavored with the cranberries that, among other things, make the Cape famous. There is some truth to the legend that enough of these drinks will make you think you saw the white whale.

2 oz rum
4 oz cranberry juice
½ cling peach
½ oz grenadine
Orange slice
Cherry

Blend ingredients with ice until frozen. Serve in a fourteen-ounce wine glass and garnish with an orange slice and cherry.

❖ HOT BUTTERED RUM ❖

The wonderful, traditional soother for cold winter nights and the nightly winter colds. Serve it piping hot in a mug that can take the heat and has a handle.

2 oz rum
1 tsp sugar
1 slice butter
Boiling water
Cinnamon stick or powdered cinnamon

Place rum and sugar in an eight-ounce mug and fill to within a half inch of the top with boiling water. Float the butter. Use a cinnamon stick for garnish, or shake powdered cinnamon on top.

❖ HURRICANE ❖

1 oz dark rum
1 oz light rum
1 oz passion fruit juice
½ oz lime juice
½ tsp sugar

Shake all ingredients with ice and strain into a cocktail glass, or serve over ice in an old-fashioned glass.

❖ IRRESISTIBLE COCKTAIL ❖

2 oz rum
1 oz sweet vermouth
1 tsp Bénédictine
½ tsp lemon juice

Shake and strain into a cocktail glass or over ice in an old-fashioned glass.

❖ JADE ❖

A refreshingly green drink that is hard to resist on hot days. It can be made short or long as indicated below.

1½ oz rum
¾ oz green crème de menthe
¾ oz orange curaçao or triple sec
¾ oz lime juice
Lime slice

Shake with ice and strain into a cocktail glass. Decorate with a lime slice. If you want a long tall variation on this for hot summer days, use a collins glass filled with ice and top with soda.

❖ KNICKERBOCKER SPECIAL ❖

After you've tried this, see Knickerbocker Cocktail under gin drinks. But don't get your hopes up.

2 oz rum
1 tsp raspberry juice
1 tsp lemon juice (or lime)
1 tsp orange juice
1 tsp curaçao or triple sec
Pineapple slices

Shake with ice, strain into a cocktail glass, and garnish with a piece of fresh pineapple.

❖ LOUISIANA LULLABY ❖

2 oz dark rum
2 tsp Dubonnet
3 drops of Grand Marnier (don't count too carefully!)
Lemon twist

Stir with ice. Serve in a cocktail glass with a lemon twist.

❖ MAI TAI ❖

Like the Zombie, this drink has a mystique born out of the infinite number of ways to make it, leaving things in, leaving things out, deciding whether or not a mimosa blossom will float on top.

1 oz light rum
1 oz dark rum
½ oz curaçao or 1 oz orange juice
Juice of 1 lime
1 tbsp orgeat or almond-flavored syrup
1 oz triple sec
2 dashes of grenadine
½ tsp sugar
Lime, lemon, and orange slices
Pineapple chunks
Maraschino cherry
Sprig of mint

The easiest way to mix this is to throw everything except the chunks of fruit into a blender and plug it in. Pour into a collins glass filled with ice and decorate with as many of the pieces of fruit as seems reasonable. One variation withholds the dark rum until everything is in place (i.e., blended and then float the dark rum on the top).

❖❖❖ MARTIAN TWEETIE ❖❖❖

Let's hope Sylvester the Cat is not imbibing at the rotating Sundial Lounge atop the Westin Peachtree Plaza in Atlanta. If he is, he's outnumbered. Here, a favorite novelty drink is the Martian Tweetie, a rum and fruit juice drink served in a Martian Tweetie glass that resembles a more ferocious version of the cartoon character who "taught he taw a puddy tat."

½ oz dark rum
½ oz light rum
½ oz passion fruit syrup
½ oz mai tai mix
⅓ oz or 1 tsp honey
2 tsp coconut milk

Blend all ingredients with ice in an electric blender. Serve on the rocks in any birdlike glass.

❖ MISSISSIPPI PLANTER'S PUNCH ❖

Not to be mistaken for its tamer siblings, Planter's Punch No. 1 and Planter's Punch No. 2, or any other Planter's Punch for that matter, the Mississippi Planter's Punch is buoyed up with bourbon and brandy.

1 oz rum
1 oz bourbon
1 oz brandy
1 oz lemon juice
1 tbsp sugar
Soda

Shake spirits, lemon juice, and sugar with ice, and strain into a collins glass filled with ice cubes. Top with soda and stir.

❖ NEVADA ❖

1½ oz rum
1 oz grapefruit juice
½ oz lime juice
2–3 tsp sugar
Dash of bitters

Shake all ingredients with ice. Serve up in a cocktail glass or over ice in an old-fashioned glass.

❖ PIÑA COLADA ❖

First concocted in a quaint little bar on a winding cobbled street in Old San Juan in the 1960s, the Piña Colada has become popular in bars as far away as London and Montreal. Best served on the beach in a half hollowed-out pineapple husk or, on more formal occasions, an electric blender can turn the drink into a refreshingly cool slush.

3 oz rum
3–4 tbsp pineapple juice
3–4 tbsp crème de coconut
Pineapple pieces

Shake with ice or place in a blender with crushed ice. Pour over ice in a collins glass; serve with a straw. Add the pieces of pineapple for garnish.

❖ PLANTER'S PUNCH ❖

Like most famous drinks, there are several variations of this. During langourous afternoons on the veranda, you can experiment to determine how fruity you like it.

2 oz Jamaican rum
1 oz lime juice
3 oz orange juice
1 tsp sugar
1 tsp triple sec
Soda
Orange slice
Cherry

Shake rum, juices, sugar, and triple sec with ice, and pour into a collins glass filled with ice. Add a squirt of soda. Garnish with an orange slice and cherry. Some recipes call for a teaspoon of pineapple juice and/or a teaspoon of lemon juice.

❖ POLYNESIA ❖

1½ oz rum
1½ oz passion fruit juice
1 tsp lime juice
1 egg white
Lime slice and cherry

Mix all ingredients in a blender with ice for ten to fifteen seconds. Serve in a champagne glass. Garnish with a lime and cherry.

❖ SHANGHAI COCKTAIL ❖

1½–2 oz rum
1 tsp anisette
1 tsp grenadine
Juice of ¼ lemon

Shake well with ice. Serve up in a cocktail glass.

❖ SLOPPY JOE'S COCKTAIL ❖

1 oz rum
1 oz dry vermouth
½ tsp curaçao
½ tsp grenadine
Juice of 1 lime

Shake with ice. Serve up in a cocktail glass.

Liquor is not a necessity. It is a means of momentarily side-stepping necessity.
CLIFTON FADIMAN

❖❖❖ SQUEEZINS ❖❖❖

This original drink from the Verandah Lounge at the Colony Square Hotel in Atlanta has the kind of name you wish you had thought of. According to the folks in Atlanta, the "carefully Squoze lemonade, rum and a smidgen of grenadine creates a taste so tart it'll have you squeezin' your lips, shaking your hips and doing flips." For that authentic southern touch, a Squeezins should be served in a Mason jar.

1 oz rum
1½ oz sour mix
½ oz grenadine
Orange wheel
Lemon wheel
Cherry

Blend all ingredients with ice in a mixer. Serve in a Mason jar either on the rocks or without ice. Garnish with the fruit wheels and the cherry.

❖❖❖ TAPA PUNCH ❖❖❖

They've been drinking Tapa Punch for almost thirty years at the Hilton Hawaiian Village where it was created by Harry Yee, the head bartender in 1958 for the Tapa Showroom. You may have to serve it in something other than the original Tapa Punch container and the miniature umbrella that decorates it.

½ oz lime juice
½ oz peach brandy
½ oz Jamaican rum
1 oz golden rum
Sweet sour mix
Pineapple wedge and cherry

Fill a tall twelve-to-fourteen-ounce glass with crushed ice. Build the drink with the first four ingredients in the order given. Top with the sweet sour mix. Garnish with the pineapple and a cherry and a miniature umbrella if you have one.

❖ TOM AND JERRY ❖

A drink invented by a swashbuckling pioneer bartender named Jerry Thomas in the famous Planters House in St. Louis in the middle of the nineteenth century. This is a very satisfying hot drink for cold nights or when you want to induce drowsiness in a sweet mellow way.

2 oz dark rum
2 oz brandy
⅓ cup hot milk
1 egg separated
1 tsp sugar
Nutmeg

Beat the egg white until stiff and the yolk until it becomes thick and syrupy. Combine the two and whip in the sugar. Put the egg mixture in a warm mug and add the brandy and rum. Fill with hot milk. Stir and sprinkle the top with nutmeg.

❖ WEST INDIAN PUNCH ❖

2 qt rum
1 fifth crème de banane
1 qt pineapple juice
1 qt orange juice
½ cup sugar (to taste)
1 tsp nutmeg
1 tsp cinnamon
1 tsp grated cloves
Soda
Sliced bananas, orange slices, and pineapple chunks

Mix sugar and spices in soda or tonic. Pour in a large punch bowl and add rum and juices. Stir. Garnish with the fruit and serve.

❖ YARD OF FLANNEL ❖

This drink was a favorite method of keeping warm in the eighteenth century. Another method, of course, was to wear a lot of flannel.

1 cup rum
1 qt ale
4 eggs
4 tbsp sugar
1 tsp grated nutmeg
1 tsp ground ginger

Beat the eggs and sugar, then add nutmeg, ginger, and rum. Heat the ale, but do not boil. Then slowly pour the hot ale into the egg mixture, stirring constantly to prevent curdling. When the ingredients are well mixed, pour the entire concoction from one pitcher to another to enhance the smooth creaminess of the drink, and then serve in warm mugs.

❖ ZOMBIE ❖

No one has ever successfully memorized the recipe for this drink. If you know any one who has, beware!

1½ oz golden rum
½ oz Jamaican rum
3 tbsp lime juice
3 tbsp orange juice
1 tbsp pineapple juice
1 tbsp papaya or passion fruit juice
1 tsp sugar
(There may be other ingredients besides these, but at the moment we can't think of them.)

Mix in a blender and pour over ice in as tall a glass as you need. Floating 151 proof rum on top is a nice touch. Some people top the floating rum slick with a little sprinkle of sugar. Some don't. The question of garnish depends a lot on gravity and the altitude you are at. Play it by ear. Zombie lovers who favor fruit garnishes usually require enormous amounts of it. The more outlandish, the better. If there is room for it, a straw is optional. If there is absolutely no room for it, a straw is essential.

TEQUILA

It's been called "bottled lightning." It's been thought to be hallucinogenic. It's supposed to come from a cactus. Some people claim it can be reactivated the "morning after" simply by drinking water. It is none of these. It is tequila.

When the Spanish conquistadores arrived in Mexico, they discovered the Aztecs' native drink called *pulque*, which was made from an agave plant. Like many Aztec customs, the Spanish found *pulque* repulsive. It tasted bitter and sour, and even back then it didn't live up to its reputation. It was too weak to really "tie one on." Undaunted, the Spanish experimented with other agave plants (there are about four hundred different types!) and eventually hit upon one that produced a drink that had more potability and potency. The new drink was called *mezcal* after the Aztec word for the plant. In time the new drink was known as mezcal wine.

In 1873 the first recorded shipment of mezcal wine entered the United States coming from the town of Tequila, just northwest of Guadalajara, a region in which the blue agave grows in great abundance. Today, both the name tequila and the use of only the blue agave are what makes tequila tequila. And by law, tequila must come from the blue agave region around Tequila. It's something like the restriction and controls on cognac in France. In the early years of World War I American soldiers fighting Pancho Villa back and forth across the American-Mexican border discovered tequila and, like the English soldiers first tasting gin in the Netherlands, brought back a liking for the curious drink.

But it was not until the mid-twentieth century that Southern California really thrust tequila to the forefront of the American drinker's consciousness. In the 1960s when Americans were searching for new life styles, it was not unusual for them to discover a new alcoholic beverage. For a while confusion over the word mezcal and mescaline, which comes from a cactus called mescal, led some Americans to think that tequila had hallucinogenic properties, and they mistook ordinary drunkenness for mystical highs, visions, and spiritual transformation. The old hangover, however, soon disspelled that myth. More enlightened tequila drinkers also learned that the agave is not a cactus at all, but a type of aloe plant. Another drink, called mezcal, is an agave beverage too, very similar to tequila, but it is not made with the blue agave. Mezcal is easily recognizable from the hideous agave worm that is included in every bottle, an unsightly creature that lives in the agave plant and is purported to act as an aphrodisiac when swallowed.

The Tequila region of Mexico grows its lucrative plants, the blue agave, on large commercial farms. Plants are harvested when they are eight or ten years old. Their juicy cores, called piña, some weighing over one hundred pounds, are then baked. When the starch converts into sugar, the piña is squeezed, the resulting liquid is called *aguamiel,* meaning honey water in English. Next the *aguamiel* is fermented with yeast and sugarcane, distilled twice, and aged. Colorless tequila receives very little aging. Gold tequila is aged in barrels and colored with caramel. Añejo tequila is the smoothest and most mellow and may have been aged up to three years.

Like its pale siblings, gin and vodka, tequila blends well with fruit juices, other beverages, and carbonated mixes. The Margarita is perhaps the most famous tequila cocktail in song and popular romance. But the Tequila Sunrise is also a favorite as are the gin drinks that tequila lovers convert into Mexican versions, such as Tequinis and Tequonics. Even the Bloody Mary must now share the brunch menu with Bloody Marias.

There is also the chest-thumping dare to "do" tequila neat. Called *Los Tres Cuates*—The Three Chums—the ritual involves licking salt from the crook of your thumb and index finger while holding a wedge of lime. It's best to follow the instructions of the one who is daring you. Either lick the salt, swig the tequila (always from the bottle), and chomp into the lime . . . or suck the lime, gulp the tequila, and then lick the salt. Proof that you passed the test is that when you finish (no matter how bad it tasted), you smile and make some comment about wanting to do it again.

❖ ACAPULCO ❖

Another version of this drink is made without tequila and pineapple. Yes, it tastes very different, but it still has the same name. See Acapulco under rum drinks.

1½ oz tequila
1½ oz rum
4 oz pineapple juice
1 tbsp lime juice
Pineapple wedges

Mix all ingredients in a shaker with ice cubes. Strain into a collins glass with ice. Garnish with fresh pineapple.

❖ AMBASSADOR ❖

2 oz tequila
Orange juice
Orange slice

Pour tequila into a tall or short glass as you prefer, on the rocks. Add orange juice and stir. Garnish with a slice of orange.

❖ AZTEC PUNCH ❖

When making strong tea for a punch, it's better to use extra tea bags rather than let the tea steep longer. When tea steeps for a long time, it acquires a tannic acidity that may conflict with the other ingredients.

2 qt tequila
2½ qt grapefruit juice
1 qt dark tea
1½ cups lemon juice
½ cup sugar or syrup
2 tsp cinnamon

Mix it any way you want.

❖ BLOODY MARIA ❖

A Mexican Bloody Mary, fiery, tantalizing, and tempestuous depending of course on how you make her.

1½ oz tequila
2 oz tomato juice
½ tsp lemon juice
½ tsp Tabasco sauce or more
Dash celery salt
Lemon Wedge

Shake with ice and strain into a highball glass with ice. Garnish with a lemon wedge.

❖ BRAVE BULL ❖

Was that a Black Russian we saw in the bull ring!

2 oz tequila
2½-3 oz Kahlúa or Tia Maria

Pour over ice in an old-fashioned glass. Stirring is optional.

❖ COCONUT SOUR ❖

2 oz tequila
Juice of ½ lemon
2 tbsp coconut milk or cream of coconut
1 tsp maraschino juice
Mix all ingredients in a blender with ice. Strain and pour into a cocktail glass.

❖ DURANGO ❖

2 oz tequila
1½ oz frozen grapefruit juice (concentrate)
½ tsp almond extract
Mineral water
Mint sprigs
Shake tequila, grapefruit juice, and almond extract with ice. Strain into a tall or short glass by preference, and top with mineral water. Decorate with sprigs of fresh mint.

❖ EARTHQUAKE ❖

2 oz tequila
1 tsp grenadine
1 tsp Cointreau or orange bitters
Orange slice
Strawberry
Mix liquid ingredients in a blender with two crushed ice cubes. Strain into a cocktail glass. Garnish with an orange slice and strawberry.

❖ ELDORADO ❖

2 oz tequila
1 oz lemon juice
1 oz orange juice
1 tbsp honey
Orange slice
Shake tequila, lemon juice, and honey very well with ice. Strain over rocks into an old-fashioned glass and garnish with an orange slice.

❖ FREDDY FUDPUCKER ❖

2 oz tequila
Galliano
Orange juice
Orange slice
Pour the tequila into a highball glass filled with ice. Add orange juice to within a half inch of the top. Stir. Float the Galliano on top. Garnish with an orange slice and serve with a straw.

❖ HOT PANTS ❖

Here is a sassy drink that is minty, fruity, sweet, and salty.

2 oz tequila
½ oz peppermint schnapps
2 tbsp grapefruit juice
1 tsp sugar
Salt

Rim a cocktail glass with salt. Shake all ingredients with ice and strain into a cocktail glass. Serve up.

❖ MARGARITA ❖

This drink has a sly way of slipping into popular song lyrics. You've probably sang about it more often than you've imbibed it. Both singing lustily about the wonders of the drink and imbibing it can raise your blood pressure. If you're prone to high blood pressure, better leave the salt off the glass and just hum along.

2 oz tequila
½ oz triple sec
Juice of ½ lime
Salt

Rim a cocktail glass with lime juice and salt. Shake tequila, triple sec, and lime juice with ice, and strain into glass. Since the saltiness encourages drinkers to consume great quantities of this drink, you might want to mix them in a blender.

❖ MAYAN WHORE ❖

This may be one of those drinks you don't want to admit you remember. It is—need we say it?—a layered drink.

1½ oz tequila
1½ oz Kahlúa
3 oz pineapple juice
Soda

Pour the tequila into an empty 8- to 10-ounce glass. Then the pineapple juice. Fill to within a half inch of the top with soda and float the Kahlúa. Add a straw and without stirring, sip gently.

❖ MONTEZUMA ❖

1½ oz tequila
1 oz madeira
1 egg yolk

Mix ingredients in a blender with about a half cup of crushed ice until it turns sloppy. Serve in a chilled champagne glass.

I only drink to make other people seem more interesting.
GEORGE JEAN NATHAN

> *You're not drunk if you can lie on the floor*
> *without holding on.*
>
> DEAN MARTIN

❖ PICADOR ❖

2 oz tequila
1 oz Kahlúa
½ tsp lemon juice
Lemon twist

Either shake with ice and strain over rocks. Or as is commonly done with Black Russians when ordered out, pour the tequila over ice and then add the Kahlúa and serve without stirring. Garnish with a lemon twist.

❖ SOUTH OF THE BORDER ❖

1½ oz tequila
1 oz coffee flavored brandy
1 oz lime juice
Lime slice

Shake with ice, and serve up in a sour glass or over ice in an old-fashioned glass. Garnish with lime slice.

❖ TEQUILA MANHATTAN ❖

It's not a real Manhattan as proven by the dash of lime juice, but then some concessions must be made to the tropical clime.

2 oz tequila
1 oz sweet vermouth
Dash of lime juice
Orange slice and cherry

Shake with ice and strain into an old-fashioned glass filled with ice. Garnish with an orange slice and cherry.

❖ TEQUILA MATADOR ❖

1 ½ oz tequila
3 oz pineapple juice
1 tsp lime juice

Shake with ice. Serve up in a champagne or cocktail glass.

❖ TEQUILA MOCKINGBIRD ❖

Not a bad drink considering the atrocious pun.

2 oz tequila
1 oz green crème de menthe
Juice of 1 lime
Lime slice

Shake with ice and strain into a cocktail glass. Hang a lime slice on the rim.

❖ TEQUILA PINK ❖

A dash of grenadine will turn the "Tequini" (the South of the Border Martini) into this lovely but still potent pink libation.

2 oz tequila
1 oz dry vermouth
1 tsp grenadine
Shake with ice. Serve up in a cocktail glass.

❖ TEQUILA PUNCH ❖

The tequila actually gets lost in the wine and champagne, but like most good punches, it will eventually sneak up on you.

1 qt tequila
2 bottles champagne
3 bottles sauterne
Sugar
2 qt melons cut in cubes or balls
Mix in a punch bowl, sweeten to taste. Chill and ice just before serving.

❖ TEQUILA STRAIGHT ❖

Known as *Los Tres Cuates*—The Three Chums—this is the way you drink it on the beach or sitting on the curb in the *zocalo*. As described in the introduction to this chapter, it really doesn't matter what order you take the three chums. The important thing is to take them quickly and claim there was nothing to it.

Instructions: Place salt on the crook between your thumb and index finger.

In the same hand, hold a wedge of lime.

In the other hand, firmly clasp a bottle of tequila.

Now... go for it!!

❖ TEQUILA SUNRISE ❖

2 oz tequila
4 oz orange juice
¾ oz grenadine

Bartenders disagree on the best way to see this sunrise. One way is to pour the grenadine into a highball glass and then fill it with ice. Add tequila and orange juice in that order. Slowly stir and watch the rosy color ascend. Others simply shake all ingredients with ice and strain into an old-fashioned glass with ice. This appeals to people who never rise early and don't believe in the sunrise. A third alternate is to mix the tequila and orange juice together. Then pour over rocks. Add grenadine slowly and let it settle before stirring. But this way is like catching the sunset and waiting through the night for dawn.

❖ TEQUINI ❖

Yes, it's a Martini made with tequila. An olive or lemon twist will help it look more like its bastardized namesake.

2 oz tequila
½ oz dry vermouth
Dash of bitters

Stir with ice, and strain into a cocktail glass or over the rocks in an old-fashioned glass.

❖ TEQUONIC ❖

2 oz tequila
Tonic
Lemon or lime wedge

Pour tequila into a highball glass with ice. Top with tonic. Squeeze the lemon or lime wedge, drop it in, and stir.

❖ TOREADOR ❖

1 ½ oz tequila
1 oz crème de cacao
1 tbsp heavy cream
Whipped cream
Cocoa powder

Shake tequila, crème de cacao, and heavy cream with ice, and strain into a cocktail or champagne glass. Add whipped cream and sprinkle with cocoa to taste.

❖ VIVA MARIA ❖

2 oz tequila
1 oz lime juice
1 egg white
1 tbsp maraschino juice
1 tsp grenadine
Lemon slice and cherry

Shake ingredients with ice, and strain into a champagne or wine glass filled with crushed ice. Garnish with fruit.

❖ VIVA VILLA ❖

With a name like Villa, this drink should have more wallop than the salty Margarita. But actually it's a less potent and sweeter drink. Still, it should satisfy the drinker who fancies the salt-rimmed glass.

1 ½–2 oz tequila
1 tsp sugar
Juice of 1 lime
Salt

Shake with ice and strain over ice into an old-fashioned glass that has been rimmed with lime juice and salt.

WINE

In vino veritas. In wine there is truth. Now the truth is, you don't need to know very much about wine for the recipes in this book. Wine cocktails and punches require very little expertise in wine selection—nothing comparable to the anxiety one must go through in choosing the right wine for the right occasion and coordinating it with the menu, determining the best sequence for wines, knowing how much to pay for a bottle of what, factoring in the need to impress your guests, and remembering which were the "very good years" and where those good years took place. Relax! For most wine cocktails and wine punches you can easily get by with what the French call *vin ordinaire.* The whole truth about wine can and does fill volumes. Wines are so various. Their descriptions are so complex: fresh, fruity, assertive, retiring, unobtrusive, imperious, friendly, forceful, intense, noblesse, lackluster, and flat. Wines can have finesse, balance, astonishing power, lusty warmth, full-bodied roundness, opulent firmness, astonishing virility, and mature earthiness. Some wines remind you of the kind of people you'd like to meet.

Glamor and romance aside, being able to spot a red or white wine and knowing a sweet from a dry wine will make you an expert on wine drinks. After all, a romantic rendezvous or an intimate evening together does not really depend on the Chardonnay, the Pinot Noir, the Cabernet Sauvignon. No, when you share a wine cocktail with someone you love or throw together a hearty wine punch for a party, noblesse, finesse, or earthiness is in the glass of the beholder, not the bottle of wine.

But here are some guidelines for making the recipes in this chapter.

In general, you can experiment with different wines. If a recipe calls for a particular wine—usually nothing more complex than white, red, sweet, or dry— sometimes a different wine will contribute an interesting variation. Keep in mind that a dry wine is less sweet and often therefore necessary in recipes containing other exceptionally sweet ingredients to avoid a cocktail that is lip-puckeringly saccharine. Also, color can be important. A red wine will distort the color of other ingredients, a white wine less so.

Champagne cocktails are always luxurious, perfect for the elegant morning brunch or a zesty drink before dinner. The bubbles that dance to the surface and the tingly fizz that tickles the nose is half the fun of drinking champagne. Don't hide the bubbly effect or the sparkling colors of champagne cocktails by using a tinted glass. Use crystal clear glasses. Here's a trick to prolong the bubble display: use a tall narrow rimmed glass, rather than a broad, flat champagne glass. The taller glass will trap the bubbles and the drink will fizz longer. Popping the cork on a champagne bottle is adventurous and heroic, but—warning!—guess what happens when you put champagne into a blender? Astonishing ballistic obtrusiveness. Don't.

Sherry is a complicated blended wine, fortified with brandy, and for this reason, sounds potent. It's not. Sherry has low alcoholic content, about 15 to 18 percent. It's not the drink to get you "ripped." So depending on your ultimate hopes for the evening, you may not want to serve your special friend a sherry cocktail. On the other hand, you might. Likewise, sherry makes a weaker party punch than one made with hard liquor. Also, sherry and port are sweet and have an "assertive" flavor. When mixed in cocktails or punches, they can really stand out.

Vermouth is technically a treated wine, consisting of an array of herbal ingredients. The Romans made vermouth by adding various roots, barks, beans, and seeds to flavor their imperious wines and act as preservatives for the long journeys on the road. The Romans were on the road a lot. Vermouth, of course, is most commonly used as a mixer with base liquors, but there are some intriguing vermouth drinks in themselves, some wine cocktails that call for vermouth, and some people enjoy certain vermouth, such as Dubonnet, on the rocks.

Yes, there is wine, and there is wine. But never does wine *ordinaire* take on such boon companions as it does in a finely wrought cocktail. Try the ones in this chapter, experiment with variations, and concoct your own wine delights for your friends. As Horace wrote:

"The wine that's waiting for you, here in my house,
Is long since mellow, and there are roses
For your hair, and balsam. Come soon."

How to Open a Champagne Bottle

The very act of opening a champagne bottle is festive, suspenseful, and dramatic. Seeing the chilled, foil-wrapped bottle quickens the pulse; holding your breath as the wire is unwound and the cork pushed upward, creates a feeling of excitement; and the loud successful pop of the cork releases the built-up emotion as it fires up toward the ceiling. Often there are cheers and applause. But is all this really necessary? No. In fact, most professional wine masters will tell you that is the wrong way to open champagne. The whole process should be discreet and muffled with no ceiling-cracking pop of the cork. Here is the more "civilized" way to open a bottle of champagne:

• First, remove the foil around the neck and unwind the wire that holds the cork in place.

• Tilt the bottle away from you slightly as it sits in the bucket of ice.

• Place a napkin over the cork so that it will not fly out when released.

• Twist the cork with your right hand in a counter-clockwise direction while turning the bottle in a clockwise direction. Do this slowly.

• As the cork eases out of the bottle, the pop should be muffled in the napkin which prevents it soaring out of your grasp.

If the cork is extremely tight and doesn't seem to want to budge, go around it with your thumb, pushing upward until it begins to loosen. Don't push it too much out of the bottle or it may get away from you. Once it is looser, proceed to rotate the bottle and cork in opposite directions as explained above.

If the cork breaks off before you can extract it completely from the bottle, insert a heavy long needle or a skewer into it to release the gaseous pressure behind it. Then remove the needle or skewer, and extract the cork as you would from a wine bottle with a corkscrew.

How to Pour Champagne

Champagne is extremely effervescent. The first glass poured from a freshly opened bottle can end up all bubbles. Some people actually pass up the first pouring for fear they'll get cheated. For when the bubbles subside, the glass may not even be a quarter full. Here's a simple way to prevent that. Pour just a little into the first glass, let the bubbles calm down, and then continue pouring slowly. A simple maneuver such as this is a courteous sign to your guest that you know the first one served runs the risk of not getting a full glass or risks the embarrassment of having to ask the host for "a little more, please."

After pouring each glass, turn the bottle slightly as you pull it away from the glass. This will prevent the last drop from rolling down the outside of the bottle. When performed deftly, that last drop hanging there on the lip should roll back up and into the bottle. Preserving the last drop is more a question of neatness and showmanship than parsimony!

No government could survive without champagne. Champagne in the throats of our diplomatic people is like oil in the wheels of an engine.

JOSEPH DARGENT

❖ ADONIS ❖

Here is a classical cocktail that is perfect as an apéritif. Something like a Manhattan, but not as heavy before a meal.

2 oz dry sherry
1 oz sweet vermouth
Dash of bitters

Stir all ingredients with ice, and strain into a cocktail glass up or over ice in an old-fashioned glass.

❖ THE BISHOP ❖

1 bottle red wine
1 tbsp honey
1 tsp allspice
2 tsp brandy
1 large orange
10 cloves

Stick cloves into the orange and bake in the oven at low temperature for half an hour. Quarter the baked orange and simmer over low heat for twenty minutes with all the other ingredients. Serve in warm cups.

Here's a version that doesn't require orange, cloves, and ovens.

Red wine
1 tsp lemon juice
1 tsp orange juice
1 tsp sugar

Shake the juice and sugar with ice. Strain into a highball glass or an old-fashioned glass with one or two ice cubes.
Fill with red wine.

Claret is the liquor for boys; port for men; but he who aspires to be a hero must drink brandy.

—SAMUEL JOHNSON

❖ BURGUNDY COCKTAIL ❖

3 oz burgundy
1 oz brandy
1 tsp maraschino juice
Lemon slice or cherry

Stir ingredients with ice, and strain into a cocktail or champagne glass. Garnish with a slice of lemon or a cherry.

❖ CARIBBEAN CHAMPAGNE ❖

This champagne cocktail has a heavy tropical flavor from the rum and crème de banane, a very restorative drink after you've been in the sun.

Champagne
1 tsp rum
½ tsp crème de banane
Banana wheel

Pour rum and liqueur into a champagne glass. Top with champagne and stir. Place a slice of banana in for garnish.

❖ CHAMPAGNE COCKTAIL ❖

The classic Champagne Cocktail—sugar, bitters, and a twist of lemon, topped with champagne.

Champagne
1 tsp sugar
2 dashes bitters
Lemon twist

Place sugar and bitters in a champagne glass. Fill with champagne. Add a twist of lemon peel for garnish.

❖ CHAMPAGNE NORMANDE ❖

This refreshing cocktail is made with calvados, an apple brandy made in the region of Normandy. Calvados is a *departement* of the French government and is supposed to be named after a galleon from the Spanish Armada that was wrecked on the coast of Normandy as it fled Sir Francis Drake. Just one of the many mishaps in that ill-fated venture.

Champagne
1 tbsp Calvados
½ tsp sugar
Dash bitters
Orange slice

Stir Calvados, sugar, and bitters in a champagne glass until the sugar is dissolved. Top with champagne. Garnish with an orange slice.

I'm only a beer teetotaller, not a champagne teetotaller.
—GEORGE BERNARD SHAW

❖ CHAMPAGNE PUNCH ❖

Add the champagne last to this punch and stir well but not to the point where all the effervescence vanishes. When first served, guests will enjoy seeing the bubbles.

2 bottles champagne
1 pt brandy
1 pt soda
1 cup triple sec
1 cup maraschino juice
Juice of 1 dozen lemons
Sugar
Seasonal fruits

Squeeze juice from lemons and sweeten with sugar to taste. Add remaining ingredients and ice. Stir well. Decorate with fruit pieces floating in punch.

❖ COCOMACOQUE ❖

Burgundy
1½ oz rum
2 oz orange juice
2 oz pineapple juice
1 tbsp lemon juice
Pineapple slice

Shake all ingredients, except the burgundy, with ice and strain into a collins glass filled with ice. Top with burgundy and garnish with a slice of pineapple.

❖ COOL CUCUMBER ❖

This drink requires a modicum of self-control. After it's prepared and stirred, you should wait a few minutes to let the cucumber flavor diffuse throughout the drink.

Champagne
1½ oz Bénédictine
¾ oz lemon juice
Cucumber strip

Pour Bénédictine and lemon juice over three ice cubes in a highball glass. Insert the cucumber strip. Fill with champagne and stir with the cucumber.

❖ DAMN THE WEATHER ❖

1½ oz red wine
¾ oz pineapple juice
¾ oz orange juice
½ tsp lemon juice
Soda
Orange, lemon, and/or pineapple slices

Shake the wine and juices with ice, and strain into a highball glass with ice. Top with soda. Garnish with fruit and drink through two straws.

❖ DEVIL'S COCKTAIL ❖

Devilishly simple!

1½ oz red wine
1½ oz dry vermouth
½ tsp lemon juice
Stir with ice. Serve up in a cocktail glass.

❖❖❖ DORCHESTER COUPE ❖❖❖
AUX FRAISES

When strawberries are in season, try this coupe aux fraises the way it is prepared at the Dorchester Bar in the Dorchester Hotel in London. When strawberries are not in season, let your imagination play with whatever fruit is available and experiment on your own. Of course it won't be a coupe aux fraises, nor an authentic "Dorchester."

Champagne
White wine
Brandy
Grand Marnier
Strawberries
Fresh mint
Marinate three or four strawberries in a little brandy and Grand Marnier for several hours. Place them in a champagne glass and top with champagne and white wine. Garnish with fresh mint.

❖ DUBONNET COCKTAIL ❖

For people who enjoy the bittersweet taste of Dubonnet, this cocktail with gin and bitters makes a fine apéritif in the late afternoon.

2 oz red Dubonnet
1 oz gin
Dash bitters
Lemon twist
Stir with ice. Serve up in a cocktail glass. Garnish with a twist of lemon.

❖ DUBONNET FIZZ ❖

The Dubonnet Fizz is a sweeter, juicier drink than the Dubonnet Cocktail. Served in a tall glass and topped with soda, it becomes a great thirst quencher on a hot, dry afternoon—or a steamy summer evening.

2 oz red Dubonnet
1 oz cherry brandy
1½ oz orange juice
½ tsp lemon juice
Soda
Shake Dubonnet, brandy, and juices with ice, and strain into a highball glass over two ice cubes. Top with soda, stir, and serve.

❖ EAST AND WEST ❖

¾ oz red wine
¾ oz brandy
¾ oz orange curaçao or triple sec
1 tbsp lemon juice
Orange and lemon slices

Shake all ingredients with ice and strain into an old-fashioned glass filled with crushed ice. Garnish with fruit slices and serve with a short straw.

❖ FIG LEAF ❖

You can adjust the amount of lime juice in this before-dinner drink to suit your taste. For those who favor the vermouth and rum blend, reduce the lime juice to a mere dash or two.

2 oz sweet vermouth
1½ oz rum
1½ tbsp lime juice
Dash bitters

Stir all ingredients with ice and serve up in a cocktail glass.

❖ GRANADA ❖

2 oz sherry
2 oz brandy
¾ oz orange curaçao or triple sec
Tonic
Orange slice

Shake sherry, brandy, and curaçao well with ice, and strain into a highball glass with ice. Top with tonic and garnish with orange slices. Serve with two straws.

❖ HONEYDEW ❖

An elegant drink reserved for that brief season when honeydew melons are ripe and willing.

Champagne
1½ oz gin
¼ cup diced honeydew melon
1 tsp Pernod
¾ oz lemon juice

Mix everything, except the champagne, in a blender with three or four ice cubes for about ten to fifteen seconds. Pour into a large (10 oz) goblet and top with champagne. Garnish with a wedge of melon.

> *I rather like bad wine . . .*
> *one gets so bored with good wine.*
> —BENJAMIN DISRAELI

❖❖❖ JADE ❖❖❖

If you order this specialty drink at the Dorchester Bar in the Dorchester Hotel in London, it will come garnished with a piece of fresh lime cut in the shape of a Chinese hat with a green cherry perched on top of the hat. If your sculpting skills aren't up for all that, I assure you the drink is just as delicious with a piece of fresh lime cut like a piece of fresh lime. Spear it with a toothpick and attach the green cherry.

Dash of Midori
Dash of blue curaçao
Dash of lime juice
Dash of angostura bitters
Champagne
Lime slice
Green cherry

Shake Midori, curaçao, lime juice, and bitters with ice and strain into a tall champagne glass. Top with champagne. Garnish with lime and green cherry.

❖ LOVING CUP ❖

These tasty wine cocktails can be made with champagne, cider, and most wines, claret being a favorite of many.

1 pt red wine (claret preferably)
3 oz brandy
2 oz triple sec
6 oz soda
4 tsp sugar (or to taste)
Mint sprigs
Seasonal fruit

Stir all ingredients in a pitcher with ice and add fruit, placing the sprigs of mint on top of the fruit. Serve in stemmed wine glasses.

❖ MIMOSA ❖

A pleasant drink that has nudged its way into the company of Screwdrivers and Bloody Marys with the brunch set. The recipe below will make a pitcher that serves about four.

1 bottle champagne
8 oz orange juice

Pour the orange juice into a pitcher and add champagne. Stir and serve in champagne glasses.

❖ MONTMARTRE ❖

A drink that conjures up visions of the romantic nightlife in that old section of Paris for which it has been named.

Champagne
1½ oz brandy
¾ oz yellow Chartreuse
1 tsp lemon juice
Dash of bitters
Cherry

Shake everything, except the champagne, with ice and strain into an old-fashioned glass. Top with champagne. Garnish with a cherry. Serve with a short straw.

❖ MULLED WINE ❖

The following recipe makes one mug. If you make this drink on a cold wintry night before the fire, you must try the traditional method of heating the ingredients by inserting a glowing poker into the mug and stirring until it reaches the boiling point.

5 oz red wine
Juice ½ lemon
1 tsp sugar
Dash bitters
½ tsp cinnamon
½ tsp nutmeg

Mix all ingredients in a small sauce pan and warm to boiling point over low heat. Stir while warming. Serve in a mug.

Here is an expanded recipe for a party. Serves about six people.

2 bottles red wine
½ bottle brandy
1 orange peel
1 lemon peel
1 tbsp nutmeg
1 tbsp ground cloves
1 tbsp cinnamon
1 tbsp sugar

Place all ingredients in a large cauldron, bring to a boil, stirring with a wooden spoon. Simmer four or five minutes. Serve piping hot in mugs.

❖ NEW ORLEANS DANDY ❖

Champagne
2 oz rum
¾ oz peach brandy
1 tsp orange juice
1 tsp lime juice
Orange slice and cherry

Shake everything, except the champagne, with ice and strain into a highball glass. Top with champagne and garnish with a slice of orange and cherry.

For filled with (wine), suffering mankind forgets its grief; from it comes sleep; with it oblivion of the troubles of the day. There is no other medicine for misery.

—EURIPIDES

*When men drink, then they are rich and successful
and win lawsuits and are happy and help their friends.
Quickly, bring me a beaker of wine, so that I may
wet my mind and say something clever.*
—ARISTOPHANES

❖PINK CALIFORNIA SUNSHINE❖

Florida orange growers might object to this name, and you might indeed find the obvious variation of the name in the southern part of the country.

*Pink champagne
Orange juice
Dash crème de cassis*

Fill a flat, saucer champagne glass with equal parts orange juice and champagne. Then add the cassis. It's best to use chilled champagne and orange juice and even a chilled champagne glass.

❖ROMAN HOLIDAY❖

*White wine
1 oz gin
¾ oz sweet vermouth
Dash lemon juice
Lemon twist*

Shake gin, vermouth, and lemon juice with ice. Strain into an old-fashioned glass without ice. Top with wine. Twist the lemon peel over the drink, rim the glass, and drop it in.

❖SANGRIA❖

There are many recipes for sangria. This one requires macerating the fruit for two hours in a syrupy mixture. If you haven't the time or the patience, of course, the fruit can be added fresh immediately before serving, but it's not as much fun to eat if it hasn't been thoroughly soaked in the sweet macerate.

*1 bottle red wine
2 oz brandy
1 oz curaçao
1 orange thinly sliced
1 apple thinly sliced
1 lime thinly sliced
½ cup sugar
1 cup cold water*

Mix the sugar and water over low heat until the sugar is dissolved and the syrupy mixture reaches the boiling point. Add the fruit and allow to marinate for two hours. Stir the remaining ingredients together in a pitcher. When ready to serve, add the marinated fruit. Pour into large wine glasses with one or two ice cubes. Allow the fruit to fall into each glass.

❖ WINE COBBLER ❖

There are many variations of cobblers. Basically all are served on shaved or crushed ice, include plenty pieces of fruit, and are sipped through straws. Try whiskey, rum, sherry, gin, and other types of wines.

Red wine
1 tsp sugar
2 oz soda
Dash of grenadine
Seasonal fruit pieces

Place sugar, soda, and grenadine in a goblet. Fill the glass with crushed ice and top with wine. Stir and decorate with fruit pieces.
An alternative method of preparation, sworn to by many bartenders, is to place the crushed ice in first, then sugar syrup (instead of sugar and soda), grenadine, and lastly the wine. Then stir. Those who swear to it, claim it makes a great difference.

❖ WINE COOLER ❖

Coolers with wine are perfect when your guests are thirsty and wine by itself would be too heavy. Coolers can be made with other spirits as well.

White or red wine
Ginger ale
Lemon or lime wedge

Fill a collins glass with ice. Add wine and ginger ale in equal amounts to fill the glass. Squeeze the fruit wedge and drop it in. Stir.

❖ WINE SPRITZER ❖

In recent years, the term spritzer seems to have supplanted cooler in describing a tall wine and carbonated beverage drink. Technically, the cooler is made only with ginger ale, and the spritzer is made with club soda.

Wine (red or white)
Carbonated beverage, usually soda
Lime or lemon wedge

In a collins glass with ice cubes combine the wine and carbonated beverage in roughly equal proportions or according to taste. Garnish with the lime or lemon as you prefer, or omit the garnish altogether. Ginger ale and red wine make a bright sparkling, refreshing spritzer although purists would call this a wine cooler.

And Noah he often said to his wife
when he sat down to dine,
"I don't care where the water goes
if it doesn't get into the wine."
—G. K. CHESTERTON

BRANDY

When Dutch traders brought it from the wine-producing countries of Southern Europe to their markets in the north, they called it *brandewijn*—brandy wine, or literally "burnt wine" because the fermented mash is branded or fired during the distillation process. Thus tested by fire, wine releases its true essence; and, for this reason, brandy is called the "soul of wine."

Made in every wine-producing country, brandy is fermented and distilled fruit mash, often grapes, although other fruits are used, such as apricots, peaches, cherries, and blackberries. All brandy tends to have a fruity quality in taste, some being quite heavy, others lighter. Fruit brandy must be made from extremely ripe fruit, and it can take up to twenty-five pounds of fruit to produce one bottle. If the fruit contains a pit, it too is included in the fermentation mash, but care is taken not to crush the pit or the bitter almond flavor would destroy the sweet taste. When the fruit has fermented, it is then distilled twice. Brandy made from berries requires an additional process. Because berries are low in sugar content, little or no fermentation results so they are first steeped in other spirits before distillation. The berry-based brandies are also lower proof, around 70, compared to fruit and grape brandies that can be 80 to 90 proof. A brandy made from fruit or berries, rather than grapes, tends to be sweeter in both bouquet and taste.

France was the first country to commercialize brandy, and today cognac and armagnac brandies are recognized around the world as the crème de la crème of brandies. So much so is the case with cognac, that the old saw about "every cognac is a brandy, but not every brandy is a cognac" evolved to clear up the misconceptions of the ignorant and those who would exploit the famous name to promote their own lower quality brand. Ironically, cognac has its origins in failure. In the eighteenth century, French traders discovered that wine shipped from the Cognac region did not hold up well on the long trans-Atlantic voyages to the growing markets in the New World. In fact, the grapes of the region do not render a very substantial wine due to acidity and low alcohol content. Cognac wine makers then began distilling their wines before shipment and the result was cognac brandy.

Always quick to set standards, the French codified the making of brandy and a bevy of laws and regulations resulted. For example, distillation of cognac must be finished by March 31 while the wine is still "young." All cognacs are then numbered by age from April 1. Distillation must be done in a pot still to produce a richer and denser flavor. It must then be aged in oak casks, the newer oak producing the deeper flavor, the older oak imparting a lighter, zestier flavor to cognac. Reading cognac labels is an art in itself to decipher the lettered code, to understand the various stars, and to translate the French names of special blends. Eg., VSOP, Cordon Bleu, XO, VSEP, and Napoleon (which does not mean it dates back to the Little Corporal's era and certainly not from his private wine cellar). It is all very mysterious, and some labels even announce *age inconnu*—age unknown, which should not alarm the potential buyer for fear it might be only one year old. *Age inconnu* is old. Very old.

There are wonderful legends, mystiques, and traditions surrounding the making and drinking of cognac, and although every myth is a legend, not every legend is a myth. For example, the air around the town of Cognac really is sweetly flavored due to the porous casks which emit about 3 to 5 percent of the contents. As it evaporates through the town, villagers like to think that the escaping 3 to 5 percent is the "angels' share." How much the angels actually receive, no one will ever know.

California brandies began when Franciscan missionaries brought grape seeds from Europe in the eighteenth century and began the wine growing culture of the West Coast. For a time brandy was more popular in the Wild West than whiskey, a flask on the hip almost as important for survival as a six shooter and holster. The California brandy industry, of course, ceased to exist during the Prohibition Era, which to wine makers ended none too soon and whose profits revived then none too quickly. Some began calling their California brands of brandy "cognac" in order to boost sales. The French government, as on other similar occasions, raised a diplomatic protest, reminding the Californians that by French law, no other brandy except that from the Cognac region of France may use the word "cognac." Not wishing to stir up an international incident over it, the Californians returned to making and advertising a brandy that was truly Californian.

Traditional uses for brandy have always been as an after-dinner drink, a genteel respite in mid-afternoon, and as an ingredient in cooking. Recently, mixed drinks with a brandy base have become popular. But for the purist, nothing will beat the time-honored custom of pouring a finger or two of brandy into a snifter, holding it momentarily so the heat from one's own palm warms the brandy, swirling it gently to "liberate the bouquet," and then sniffing the satisfying aroma with a long deep inhalation. Aaaaah!

❖ APPLE BRANDY SOUR ❖

Here is the basic sour drink made with apple brandy. Like all sours, this drink is perfect before a meal because its tartness does not spoil one's appetite. If you like the Apple Brandy Sour, try it with apricot brandy and regular brandy.

2 oz apple brandy
Juice ½ lemon
½ tsp sugar
Lemon slice and cherry

Shake brandy, sugar, and lemon juice with ice. Serve up or on the rocks in an old-fashioned glass. Garnish with lemon and cherry.

❖ AMERICAN BEAUTY ❖

According to Michael Jackson this cocktail soothes both the mind and the stomach because of its fine ingredients.

¾ oz brandy
¾ oz dry vermouth
½ oz white crème de menthe
1 oz orange juice
Dash of grenadine
1 tbsp port

Shake all ingredients, except the port, with ice. Strain into an old-fashioned glass with ice or serve up in a cocktail glass. Float the port on top.

❖ APPLE RUM RICKEY ❖

Rickey's lie somewhere between sours and collins. This one with apple brandy and rum is an interesting variation on the standard Rickey made with a grain spirit.

1 oz applejack
1 oz rum
Soda
Large lime wedge

Pour applejack and rum into a highball glass with ice. Fill with soda. Squeeze the lime wedge thoroughly into the drink and drop it in. Stir.

❖ APPLEJACK PUNCH ❖

Like most punches, amounts will vary depending upon the number of drinkers and the potency desired. Best to experiment. Almost any combination works.

2 bottles applejack brandy
1 cup lemon juice
1 pt orange juice
6 oz grenadine
2 bottles ginger ale
Apple slices
Sprigs of mint

Mix all ingredients, except the ginger ale, apples, and mint, with large chunks of ice in a punch bowl. Just before serving, add the ginger ale and the garnish.

❖ APPLEJACK RABBIT ❖

2 oz apple brandy
1 tsp lemon juice
1 oz lime or orange juice
1 tsp maple syrup

Rim an old-fashioned glass with maple syrup and sugar. Shake all ingredients with ice. Fill glass with ice and strain drink into it.

❖ BALTIMORE EGGNOG ❖

This eggnog is a favorite at parties. The recipe below is for one drink only, but the measurements in parentheses will make about thirty servings.

1 oz brandy (1 pt)
1 oz rum (½ pt)
1 oz madeira (½ pt)
1 egg (12)
1 tsp sugar (2 cups)
¾ cup milk or 2 oz heavy cream (3 pt)
Nutmeg

Shake with ice, and strain into a collins glass or a highball glass. If heavy cream is used, you may want to top the drink with milk. Dust the surface with lots of nutmeg.

❖ BETSY ROSS ❖

The recipe below is a "no frills" Betsy Ross. To turn this drink into a pick-me-up, add one egg yolk, one teaspoon of sugar, and two dashes of angostura bitters. Shake well, strain into a cocktail glass, and dust the top with nutmeg.

1 ½ oz brandy
1 ½ oz port
1 tsp triple sec

Shake or stir with ice, and strain into an old-fashioned glass with ice cubes.

❖ BETWEEN THE SHEETS ❖

This potent drink has the reputation for putting you right where its name suggests. If you make it that far. Those that don't are usually two sheets to the wind, but there's no drink for that. Except this one.

1 oz brandy
1 oz triple sec
1 oz rum
1 tsp lemon juice
Lemon twist

Shake with ice. Serve up in a cocktail glass. Garnish with lemon.

❖ BRANDY ALEXANDER ❖

A romantic and seductive cocktail to enhance the dreaminess of a late night, but many fans of the Brandy Alexander don't wait for the late hours. Recently it has become a popular happy hour drink for the late afternoon.

1 ½ oz brandy
1 oz dark crème de cacao
1 oz heavy cream
Nutmeg

Shake ingredients with ice. Serve up in a cocktail glass. Sprinkle the top with nutmeg.

❖ BRANDY OLD-FASHIONED ❖ COCKTAIL

The Brandy Old-fashioned Cocktail transforms the straight brandy into a more delicate libation, making it a lighter apéritif for the cocktail hour before dinner.

2 oz brandy
½ tsp sugar
2 dashes bitters
Lemon twist

Stir with ice, strain into a cocktail glass, and garnish with a lemon.

❖ BRANDY DAISY ❖

2 oz brandy
Juice ½ lemon
1 tsp sugar
1 tsp grenadine
Cherry, lemon, orange garnishes

Shake with ice, and strain into a small stein or a sour glass. One cube of ice may be added. Garnish with some combination of fruit.

Drunks are rarely amusing unless they know some good songs and lose a lot at poker.

KARYL ROOSEVELT

❖ CHERRY BLOSSOM ❖

1 oz cherry brandy
1 oz cognac
½ oz triple sec (or slightly more)
2 tsp lemon juice
Few drops of grenadine
Cherry
Maraschino juice
Powdered sugar

Rim a cocktail glass with maraschino juice and powdered sugar. Shake ingredients with ice until very cold, strain into a cocktail glass and garnish with a cherry.

❖ CHERRY FIZZ ❖

For a variation on this fizz, try topping it with champagne rather than soda!

2–3 oz cherry brandy
Juice ½ lemon
Soda
Cherry

Shake brandy and lemon juice with ice. Strain into an old-fashioned glass with ice cubes. Top with soda and add a cherry.

❖ CRÈME DE MENTHE FRAPPÉ ❖

A minty after-dinner drink that satisfies the palate and compliments a heavy spicy meal. Frappés are ideal for people who like their liqueur cold and slightly diluted.

Green crème de menthe

Fill a cocktail glass or a champagne glass with crushed ice, and add crème de menthe. Serve with two short straws.

❖ DEPTH CHARGE ❖

Also called a Depth Bomb, this drink might make a hit on a submarine!

1 ½ oz brandy
1 ½ oz calvados
½ oz grenadine
1 oz lemon juice
Lemon twist

Shake ingredients, and strain into a cocktail glass or over ice in an old-fashioned glass. Decorate and flavor with a twist of lemon.

❖ FIFTH AVENUE ❖

1 oz dark crème de cacao
1 oz apricot brandy
1 oz heavy cream (or slightly less)

Pour each ingredient individually in the order given into a liqueur glass. Do this gently and do not mix, so the result is a layered drink.

❖ GEORGIA MINT JULEP ❖

1½ oz brandy
1½ oz peach brandy (or peach-flavored liqueur)
1 tsp sugar
3 sprigs mint

Muddle six to eight mint leaves in a collins glass with sugar and a little water. Add ice. Pour in brandies. Garnish with a sprig of mint.

❖ HARVARD COCKTAIL ❖

The Harvard Cocktail is not a variation on the Yale Cocktail listed under gin drinks. It's a whole different ball game.

1½ oz brandy
¾ oz sweet vermouth
2 tsp lemon juice
1 tsp grenadine
Dash bitters

Shake all ingredients with ice. Serve up in a cocktail glass.

❖ KISS IN THE DARK ❖

1 oz brandy
1 oz gin
1 oz dry vermouth

Stir gently with ice. Serve up in a cocktail glass.

❖ EAST INDIA ❖

2 oz brandy
1 tsp rum
½ tsp triple sec or curaçao
½ tsp pineapple juice
Dash bitters
Lemon twist and cherry

Shake all ingredients, except the fruit, with ice. Strain into a cocktail glass and decorate with the lemon twist and a cherry.

❖ LADY BE GOOD ❖

2 oz brandy
½ oz sweet vermouth
½ oz white crème de menthe

Shake with ice. Serve up in a cocktail glass.

❖ MIKADO COCKTAIL ❖

2 oz brandy
½ tsp crème de cacao
½ tsp curaçao or triple sec
Dash bitters

Shake well with ice and strain into a cocktail glass.

❖ MONTANA ❖

1½ oz brandy
1 oz red wine
1 oz dry vermouth
Pour all ingredients into an old-fashioned glass with ice and stir.

❖ PEACH SANGAREE ❖

Sangarees are like tall Old-Fashioneds served in a highball or a collins glass. Usually the liquor and sugar are muddled in the glass, but as in the Peach Sangaree, the sugar is omitted because peach brandy is rather sweet to begin with. The true trademark of a Sangaree, however, is the port floated on top and sprinkled with nutmeg.

2 oz peach brandy
1 tsp port
Soda
Nutmeg
Pour brandy into a highball glass. Fill with ice. Add soda to within a half inch from the top. Stir. Then float the port and sprinkle with nutmeg.

❖ PRAIRIE OYSTER ❖

Here's the famous eye opener guaranteed to rid you of hangover the morning after. Some people, however, claim that this cure is worse than the disease.

2 oz brandy
1 egg
1 tsp catsup
Dash Worcestershire sauce
Salt
Crack the egg and drop the unbroken egg carefully into a wine glass or an old-fashioned glass. Add the brandy, catsup, Worcestershire sauce, and salt to taste. Drinking directions: Down it in one gulp, swallowing the egg whole. Then rejoin the coffee drinkers.

❖ ❖ ❖ THE RAPHAEL KISS ❖ ❖ ❖

This Kiss comes from the Raphael Hotel in Chicago where it was invented by bartender George Way. It's a wonderful drink for anyone who likes sweet things, be they drinks or kisses or sweet nothings.

4 oz vanilla ice cream
2 oz chocolate ice cream
½ oz Kahlúa
½ oz brandy
½ oz sambuca
½ oz Half-and-Half
Lime wedge
Cinnamon and sugar mixture

In a mixer, blend the ice cream, Kahlúa, brandy, and Half-and-Half. Pour into a nine-ounce wine glass rimmed with lime juice and dipped into the cinnamon and sugar mixture. Float sambuca on top.

❖ SIDECAR ❖

Invented in Paris during World War I, the Sidecar is named after the sidecar on the motorcycle in which the army officer who popularized the drink rode to his favorite watering hole. Controversy surrounds the exact watering hole, the Rotonde, Harry's Bar, the Dome, and the Ritz all making some claim to it. The drink was brought to the United States during Prohibition where it, like many other illegal concoctions, thrived.

2 oz cognac
½ oz triple sec
½ oz lemon juice
Lemon twist

Shake the brandy, triple sec, and lemon juice with plenty of ice, and strain into a cocktail glass. Garnish with a twist of lemon peel.

❖ STINGER ❖

Tradition dictates that the Stinger be shaken not stirred, even though the two simple ingredients would suggest gentle stirring as is done in most drinks where the components are clear and blend easily.

1½ oz brandy
1 oz white crème de menthe

Shake with ice, and serve up in a cocktail glass or on the rocks in an old-fashioned glass. Substitute peppermint schnapps for the crème de menthe without any deleterious effects (to the drink).

❖ VANDERBILT ❖

1½ oz brandy
1½ oz cherry brandy
½ oz lemon juice
1 tsp sugar
2 dashes bitters

Stir with ice, and gently pour into a cocktail glass or over ice in an old-fashioned glass. Some people enjoy a twist of lemon with it.

❖ WASSAIL ❖

The traditional Yuletide party drink. Here are two recipes out of dozens.

6 oranges
1 gal apple cider
1½ cups lemon juice
12 cinnamon sticks
2 cups vodka
½ cup brandy
Whole cloves

Insert cloves into the oranges and bake at 350 degrees in a shallow pan for thirty minutes. Heat cider just to boiling point. Remove from heat and add lemon juice, cinnamon sticks, and oranges. Heat for a half hour over low heat. Add vodka and brandy immediately before serving. Serve warm in a punch bowl.

This recipe is apple and wine based rather than oranges and vodka.

12 small apples
Brown sugar
2 bottles dry sherry or other dry wine
4 cloves
1 tsp grated nutmeg
1 tsp ground ginger
1 stick cinnamon
2 cups sugar
½ cup water
6 eggs, separated
1 cup brandy

Bake the apples, cored and filled with brown sugar, in a shallow pan of water at 350 degrees for thirty minutes. Combine wine, nutmeg, ginger, cloves, sugar, and water, and heat just to boiling point. Leave on very low heat. Beat egg yolks until thick and lemon-colored. Beat the whites until stiff. Fold the whites into the yolks. Strain the mixture of wine and spices. Then pour the wine slowly into the eggs, stirring constantly. Last, add the brandy and serve in a punch bowl with the apples on top.

❖ THE WHIP ❖

1½ oz brandy
1½ oz sweet vermouth
1½ oz dry vermouth
1 tsp Pernod
1 tsp orange curaçao
Orange twist

Shake with ice and pour into a cocktail glass. Serve with a twist of orange.

❖ WIDOW'S KISS ❖

1½ oz brandy
1 oz yellow Chartreuse
1 oz Bénédictine
Dash of bitters

Shake with ice. Serve up in a cocktail glass. Sometimes this drink is garnished with a fresh strawberry.

> *Call things by their right names—Glass of brandy and water! That is the current but not the appropriate name: ask for a glass of liquid fire and distilled damnation.*
>
> —ROBERT HALL

LIQUEURS

People have been fiddling around with fruit and nuts for a long time. In the Middle Ages alchemists, witches, and monks, who had more in common than most people realize, were the professional herbalists of their day. Either for magical, medicinal, or spiritual reasons—which are not as distinguishable as many people think—herbs, roots, barks, seeds, fruit, flowers, weeds, and pits were added to neutral spirits. The result? A foul and loathesome taste as you can imagine. Eventually honey was added and it tasted better. The result? A drink that would come to be known as a liqueur in most of the world, a cordial in the United States.

Both terms go back to medieval Latin. *Liquifacere* means to dissolve; *cordis* means of the heart. In other words, the weeds and pits, etc. dissolved in neutral spirits were thought to stimulate respiration and strengthen the heart. By the sixteenth century Catherine de Medici took Italian liqueurs with her to France for her royal marriage; the Bénédictine monks were already brewing their secret recipe; and in Holland, the House of Bols was laying the foundation for a long distinguished career in the liqueur industry. As the Age of Exploration brought sugarcane, spices, fruit, and flowers from the East and West Indies, sweeter and more exotic ingredients were added to the hocus pocus of making liqueurs.

A liqueur is a neutral spirit to which is added the fruit, nuts, berries, etc. that flavor it. All are sweet, some sickeningly so; all are low in alcohol, usually 60 proof or less. A liqueur is never a straight flavor, but a blend of several or many flavoring agents. Liqueurs are not aged.

There are three main processes for making liqueurs. The flavoring agents can be mixed with the neutral spirits and then distilled. Seeds and peels are usually treated this way. Or the flavoring ingredient can be steeped in the spirit, macerated, the liquid filtered out, and the leftover mash then distilled. Fruit liqueurs are made by this process. The third method is to percolate the spirit over the flavoring ingredient, like water over coffee, until the spirit takes on the flavor. The remaining "grounds" can be distilled after the liquid is removed. This process works well on beans and pods, such as cocoa, vanilla, and, naturally, coffee.

Some liqueurs are botanical, meaning that no single flavor of any ingredient dominates the taste. It is not surprising that the more famous of these are the monastery liqueurs that were developed primarily for medicinal purposes—Chartreuse, Bénédictine, Claristine, Trappistine, and Galliano (which was named after an Italian officer in the Abyssinian War, not a monastery). Another category of liqueurs are liquor based, meaning that the base is a recognizable liquor, not a neutral spirit—Drambuie (Scotch), Irish whiskey, Southern Comfort, and Wild Turkey liqueur. In the 1970s the newest type of liqueurs were concocted—cream liqueurs—proving that there is still scope for invention and discovery in an age-old art. Usually cream and alcoholic spirits don't mix. Even the thought disgusts some people. But a blending process was discovered which holds them together in a rich, creamy, rather sweet arrangement that slides down the tongue smoothly and easily.

There is a bewildering variety of liqueurs on the market. Name your favorite fruit, berry, nut, spice, herb, bark, or root, and there's probably a liqueur somewhere that contains it. If you can't find it, you probably don't need it. When asking around, however, keep in mind that some liqueurs are generic, in that they are referred to by their primary ingredient, such as cherry liqueur, apricot liqueur, crème de cacao, peppermint schnapps. It's pretty obvious what you're asking for. Others, known as proprietary liqueurs, are named after the company, house, or monastery that makes them, such as Grand Marnier, Bénédictine, and Caffe Lolita (a U.S. firm, not a monastery) to name only a few.

Liqueurs are fun—to drink and know about. Some are steeped in legends about lost formulas and secret recipes. Supposedly during the French Revolution, the monks at Chartreuse were tortured for their famous recipe, now only three monks know it. The Bénédictine Abbey was burned during the same revolution, the formula lost, only to resurface years later. Drambuie was a personal gift from Bonnie Prince Charlie to his supporters in the Rising of '45. Irish whiskey fled to the mainland with Irish refugees, when Tudor troups invaded the Emerald Isle, and it miraculously popped up years later in Austria. Caffe Lolita was . . . Well, the stories go on and on.

❖ AMARETTO SOUR ❖

2–3 oz Amaretto
¾ oz lemon juice
Orange slice

Shake with ice, and strain into a sour glass or over the rocks in an old-fashioned glass. Unlike other sour recipes, this one will be sweet enough without the sugar. Garnish with an orange slice. Or be adventurous and try a new topping.

❖ AMARETTO STINGER ❖

2 oz amaretto
1 oz white crème de menthe

Shake well with ice. Serve up in a cocktail glass or over ice in an old-fashioned glass.

❖ ANGEL'S TIP ❖

This drink and the following, Angel's Wing, are remarkably similar in name but not in taste. The dash of brandy in the "wing" virtually transports the "tip" to the very top of perfection.

White crème de cacao
Heavy cream
Cherry

In a liqueur glass, pour the crème de cacao. Float the cream on top. Insert a toothpick through the cherry and lay it across the rim of the glass.

❖ ANGEL'S WING ❖

White crème de cacao
Heavy cream
½ oz brandy
Cherry

Pour the crème de cacao into a liqueur glass as in the previous recipe, leaving room for the cream. Float the cream. Lay the cherry with a toothpick over the rim of the glass and pour the brandy over it, letting it float down into the cream.

❖ BACKCRACKER ❖

This drink is a potent combination of the Dynasty and the Harvey Wallbanger sans vodka.

1½ oz Southern Comfort
1½ oz Amaretto
1 oz Galliano
3 oz orange juice
3 oz pineapple juice

Blend all ingredients well with ice and serve in a Hurricane glass or other tall glass with ice.

❖ BANANA BLISS ❖

1½ oz crème de banane
1½ oz white rum
1 oz orange juice
Dash of bitters
1½ oz heavy cream
2 dashes of grenadine
3 banana wheels

Shake the first five ingredients with ice and strain into an old-fashioned glass. Decorate with two dashes of grenadine and the banana slices.

❖ CAFÉ AMARETTO ❖

1 oz amaretto
1 oz Kahlúa
1 cup hot coffee
Whipped cream

Pour the liqueurs into the coffee leaving room for a generous heaping of whipped cream.

❖ CARA SPOSA ❖

1½ oz Tia Maria
1½ oz orange curaçao or triple sec
1½ oz heavy cream
Sugar
Orange slice

Blend the Tia Maria, curaçao, and cream for fifteen to twenty seconds with several ice cubes. Strain into a champagne saucer rimmed with sugar. Hang an orange slice on the side.

❖ CORCOVADO ❖

A *corcovado* is a hunchback!

1½ oz Drambuie
1½ oz blue curaçao
1½ oz tequila
Lemonade
Lemon or lime slice

Shake the spirits with ice and strain into a highball glass filled with crushed ice. Fill with lemonade. Garnish with a slice of fruit. Serve with straws.

❖ DIANA ❖

A refreshing after-dinner drink that can be turned into a frappé with crushed ice.

2 oz white crème de menthe
½ oz brandy

In a pony glass pour the crème de menthe. Float the brandy on top and serve with a steady hand.

❖ DIANA FRAPPÉ ❖

Here is a variation on the Diana made with crushed ice.
3 oz white crème de menthe (or peppermint schnapps)
3 tsp brandy
Fill a cocktail glass with crushed ice and pour on the crème de menthe. Float the brandy and serve with two small straws.

❖ DYNASTY ❖

This drink is in the "dynasty" of Godfather and Godmother drinks. Instead of Scotch and vodka respectively for the respected patriarch and matriarch of these amaretto drinks, this one is made with Southern Comfort. A southern branch of that family which makes offers you can't refuse.
1½ oz Southern Comfort
1½ oz amaretto
Stir with ice and strain into an old-fashioned glass with ice.

❖❖❖ FAIRMONT FREEZE ❖❖❖

This refreshing freeze comes from deep in the heart of Texas. It's a tasty almond ice cream drink from the Pyramid Lounge in the Fairmont Hotel in Dallas, but you don't need to be a cowpuncher or oil baron to enjoy it.
1½ oz amaretto
1 scoop vanilla ice cream
Sliced toasted almonds
Place the amaretto and ice cream in a blender and blend until thoroughly mixed. Serve in a chilled cocktail glass without ice. Sprinkle sliced toasted almonds on top.

❖ GLOOM CHASER ❖

1 oz Grand Marnier
1 oz curaçao
1 oz grenadine
1 oz lemon juice
Shake with ice. Serve up in a cocktail glass.

❖ GOLDEN CADILLAC ❖

Not everyone's dream car is a Cadillac. For a "Golden Dream" substitute a half-ounce of Cointreau and a half ounce of orange juice for the crème de cacao and see if it rides more to your liking.
1 oz Galliano
1 oz white crème de cacao
1 oz heavy cream
1 oz orange juice
Shake well with ice cubes or mix in a blender with crushed cubes of ice. Strain into a cocktail glass or a champagne glass.

LIQUEURS

❖ GRASSHOPPER ❖

Some Grasshoppers have shaved chocolate sprinkled over the top. It tastes delicious, but some people complain that it looks like spat tobacco juice. Try it, but don't think about it. For a vodka version of the Grasshopper, see The Flying Grasshopper under vodka drinks.

1 oz green crème de menthe
1 oz white crème de cacao
1 oz heavy cream
Shake with ice and strain into a cocktail glass or a champagne glass.

❖ KAHLÚA GOOD NIGHT ❖

Kahlúa
1 tsp crème de noyaux
Heavy cream
Pour Kahlúa about half way to the top of a cocktail glass filled with crushed ice. Add the crème de noyaux. Top with heavy cream.

❖ LOLLIPOP ❖

This one is not on a stick.

1 oz Cointreau
1 oz green Chartreuse
1 oz Kirsch
Dash maraschino
Shake all ingredients with ice and strain into a cocktail glass without ice.

❖ MACARONI ❖

2 oz Pernod
1½ oz sweet vermouth
Shake both ingredients with ice and strain into a cocktail glass.

❖ PETITE FLEUR ❖

1½ oz orange curaçao
1½ oz white rum
1½ oz grapefruit juice
Orange twist
Shake ingredients with ice and strain into a cocktail glass. Garnish with an orange peel.

❖ PINK SQUIRREL ❖

1½ oz crème de noyaux
1½ oz white crème de cacao
1½ oz heavy cream
Shake with ice and strain into a cocktail glass.

❖ POUSSE-CAFÉ ❖

The secret of a Pousse-Café is getting the order of the ingredients right so that their specific densities keep them floating on top of each other. You will also need a steady hand both in pouring and serving.

Crème de cassis
Chartreuse
Brandy

Pour the crème de cassis into a pousse-café glass, filling it about one-third full. Then float the Chartreuse carefully. Lastly, float brandy on the top.

❖ RADISSON SNOWBALL ❖

This Snowball comes from the desert. It was developed by Thomas Krietler, food and beverage director of the Oasis lounge in the Radisson Hotel in Scottsdale, Arizona. A delicious way to cool off on a hot day, and if Arizona doesn't know what a hot day is, no one does!

1 oz amaretto
½ oz white crème de cacao
1 tsp Cocoa Lopez
1 scoop Häagen-Dazs vanilla ice cream
2 oz Half-and-Half
½ slice fresh pineapple

Blend all ingredients with a scoop of ice. Serve in a twelve-ounce tulip glass and garnish with the slice of pineapple.

❖ RHETT BUTLER ❖

The original Rhett Butler was a notorious albeit romantic gun runner who would sell to either side to make a buck. Like its namesake, this drink has a little something to offer everyone, in the line of citric flavoring, that is.

1½ oz Southern Comfort
1 oz orange curaçao
¾ oz lime juice
¾ oz lemon juice
½ oz orange juice
Soda
Orange slice and mint sprig

Shake the liqueurs and the juices well with ice and strain into a highball glass filled with crushed ice. Top with soda and garnish with orange and mint. Serve with one or two thin straws.

❖ ROMAN SNOWBALL ❖

Keep the ingredients with you and if you get stuck in an Alpine pass in a blizzard, you won't mind all that much.

2 oz sambuca
3-4 coffee beans

Pack a wine glass three-fourths full with crushed ice and pour the sambuca over it. Stick the coffee beans into the ice and let them soak up the sambuca. When the drink is finished and you're waiting for the Saint Bernards or the rescue team, chew the beans like candy. It's important to keep moving in freezing temperatures.

❖ ❖ ❖ SECRET LOVE ❖ ❖ ❖

The Salle Bonaventure at the Queen Elizabeth Hotel in Montreal developed this drink with the alluring name. Half the fun of this drink is suggesting it to your guests. "Have you ever had a Secret Love?" The other half, of course, is drinking it.

1 oz coconut amaretto liqueur
½ oz white rum
½ oz lemon juice
1 oz orange juice
½ oz cranberry juice
Cherry

Shake ingredients with ice and strain into a cocktail glass straight up. Garnish with a cherry.

❖ SOUTHERN PEACH ❖

After you've tried the peach brandy version, experiment with other flavors. You'll find that Southern Comfort blends well with other fruits, but then, as in all things, it's a matter of taste.

2 oz Southern Comfort
1½ oz peach brandy
Dash of bitters
1½ oz heavy cream

Shake well with ice and strain into a cocktail glass or over ice in an old-fashioned glass. Try a slice of fresh peach as a garnish.

❖ VELVET HAMMER ❖

1 oz Tia Maria
¾ oz brandy
¾ oz triple sec
1½ oz heavy cream

Shake ingredients with ice and strain into a cocktail glass.

❖ YELLOW FINGERS ❖

This drink may remind you of the Backcracker or a high fallutin' Harvey Wallbanger.

1½ oz Southern Comfort
1½ oz vodka
¾ oz Galliano
1½ oz orange juice
Lemonade
Orange slice and cherry

Shake the spirits and orange juice with ice and strain into a highball glass with two cubes of ice. Top with lemonade and garnish with an orange slice and cherry.

STARTING FROM SCRATCH CHECKLIST

Here is a beginner's checklist for the novice home-bartender who is literally starting from scratch.

Liquor

☐ bourbon
☐ Scotch
☐ gin
☐ vodka
☐ rum
☐ tequila
☐ white/red wine
☐ brandy

Mixes

☐ soda
☐ cola
☐ ginger ale
☐ tomato juice
☐ sweet/dry vermouth
☐ tonic
☐ 7-Up
☐ orange juice
☐ lime juice

Other Ingredients

☐ sugar/simple syrup
☐ grenadine
☐ salt/pepper
☐ bitters
☐ tabasco sauce
☐ Worcestershire sauce

Garnishes

☐ olives
☐ pearl onions
☐ maraschino cherries
☐ fresh fruit
  (lemons, limes, oranges, etc.)

Bar Equipment

☐ shot glass
☐ shaker
☐ strainer
☐ ice bucket, tongs
☐ blender
☐ bottle opener
☐ corkscrew
☐ paring knife/cutting board
☐ juice squeezer

Essential Glassware

☐ stem cocktail glass (4 oz)
☐ old-fashioned or rocks glass (6 oz)
☐ highball glass (8 oz)
☐ collins glass (10 oz)

GLOSSARY

Absinthe A liqueur made from wormwood that causes havoc to the central nervous system. Supposedly responsible for flights of fancy, madness, uncontrollable passion, and death, it has been called a "muse in a bottle," a love potion, and an inspiration to artists such as Hemingway, Picasso, and Degas. The much too potent drink is now illegal almost everywhere, and it has been replaced by anise and Pernod, licorice- and aniseed-flavored spirits, which mix well in drinks that at one time would have called for absinthe and its dire effects.

Ale A British type of beer, often reddish or copper colored with a heavy flavor of hops making it considerably more bitter than regular beer.

Amaretto An almond-flavored liqueur, originally made in Italy in the early sixteenth century as a love gift from a model to her artist-lover. Still a drink to conclude the candlelit dinner and ease the transition from the table to the balcony to the boudoir. A popular and presumably effective brand is aptly named Amaretto di Amore.

Amer Picon A thick syrupy apértif made from oranges and gentian. Mixes well in cocktails calling for orange flavoring.

Angostura A bitter aromatic bark used in bitters with a rum base. Named after a Venezuelan town renamed Ciudad Bolivar, angostura bitters are now produced in Trinidad. Usually a dash or two is all that is needed to perk up a drink.

Anise Any aniseed flavored drink. The French term is anisette. A syrupy licorice liqueur that has replaced absinthe. Other ingredients are added, and the finished product is usually colorless, although there are some bright red variations.

Apéritif Literally, a small alcoholic drink imbibed immediately before a meal to whet the appetite. Sherry, champagne, or any cocktail that is not too heavy and filling can serve as an apéritif. From the French meaning *opening,* that is, the introduction to dinner.

Applejack In 1964 the New Jersey legislature declared unanimously that applejack, an apple brandy, was "the oldest native distilled spirit beverage in the United States." So far, no test of this has reached the Supreme Court. Most applejack is about 20 percent apple brandy distilled from hard cider and the rest is neutral spirits. Even though the history of applejack centers around New Jersey, a folk legend from New England claims that the first attempts at making applejack involved burying a cask of fermented cider in the snow during the long New England winter. When the water content of the cider had frozen, a hot poker inserted through the bung hole allowed the applejack to be poured out.

Bénédictine First made by Bénédictine monks in 1510, this liqueur is considered to be the oldest in the world. The secret recipe has survived war, revolution, and commercialization. Bénédictine requires over twenty herbs and plants, a three-year-long production process, and a subsequent four years for aging. Competitors have tried, and failed, to copy it. Undoubtedly the motto *Deo Optimo Maximo* (To God Most Good, Most Great), D.O.M., protects each bottle and the mysterious recipe as well.

Bitters An alcoholic liquid in which bitter roots, barks, and peels have been steeped to produce the tart flavor that, when used in minuscule proportions, can temper many sweet drinks. The usual flavorings are orange and peach, but there are other flavors as well.

Cacao, Crème de A chocolate flavored liqueur, either dark brown or white. There is also a vanilla-flavored version. Both are made from the cacao beans that grow on the cacao tree of South America.

Campari An Italian apéritif that has become extremely popular in America in recent years, usually mixed with soda and served on the rocks. It is also used as a flavoring agent in other cocktails. Its dry taste of quinine is not for those who enjoy a sweeter, more mellow taste.

Cassis, Crème de An alcoholic liqueur with a black currant flavor. There is also a nonalcoholic version that is actually a black currant syrup. When the black currant mash is added to neutral spirits, a wonderfully rich mixer results that goes well with white wine, champagne, vermouth, or brandy.

Chartreuse Supposedly the secret recipe for this herbal liqueur is known only by three Carthusian monks, and they aren't telling. Made from a hundred and thirty herbs, spices, and other ingredients, the liqueur has a green or yellow cast to it which according to the holy distillers is not created by any extraneous dye. The secret is over three hundred years old and well sequestered behind the cloistered walls of its caretakers.

Chaser A drink of beer, water, or some milder liquor taken fast on the heels of a more spirited liquor.

Cinzano A brand name of a vermouth manufacturer that has recently cropped up on yellow and black umbrellas over tables in outdoor cafés.

Cobbler Neither a shoemaker nor a fruit pie. A drink consisting of a liquor base, fruit, generous garnishes of berries and fresh fruit, all served on heaping amounts of shaved ice in a tall goblet.

GLOSSARY

Collins A tall cool drink served in the tallest of drink glasses with the same name. A collins glass is straight, slim and holds ten to twelve ounces. Gin and bourbon are the most popular collinses, known as Tom and John, respectively, but other base liquors can be substituted. A collins consists of liquor, lemon or lime juice, sugar, soda, lots of ice, and is garnished with a lemon slice and cherry.

Cointreau A famous brand name of triple sec, which is a clear liqueur made from orange peels.

Curaçao A liqueur made from the peels of small green oranges grown in the West Indies. Triple sec is a very dry variety made by various houses, the most famous being Cointreau. Curaçao comes in a rainbow of colors: orange, blue, green, white, and can add a splash of happiness to an exotic drink without changing the basic orange flavor.

Daisy A cocktail made with almost any liquor to which is added lemon or lime juice, grenadine, or raspberry syrup and served over one ice cube.

Drambuie A Scotch liqueur made from malt whiskey and heather-based honey. Legend has it that Bonnie Prince Charlie bequeathed his own personal recipe for Drambuie to his supporters during the Rising of 1745. In Gaelic the term means "the drink that satisfies"—*an dram buidheach.*

Dubonnet Connoisseurs claim this apéritif hugs the middle ground in the tug of war between sweet and dry vermouths. There is a slight quinine flavor to Dubonnet whether you favor the better known dark red variety or the white.

Eau de Vie French for "water of life" and it signifies—what else?—brandy! But of course!

Flip Flips are like eggnogs but are shaken so they come out frothy. Usually served over ice and sprinkled with nutmeg. A time-honored custom is to have a flip before bedtime at night. An equally time-honored custom is to have one in the morning on rising. The world is a better place because of time-honored customs.

Frappé Any liquor served straight over finely crushed ice is a frappé. Green crème de menthe is one of the most popular. Insert two short straws into this spiritous ball of ice and drink slowly and gently as it melts.

Galliano The Empire State Building of bottles on the bar rack, Galliano rises tall and proud, like its namesake, Major Giuseppe Galliano, who gallantly held off an army of Abyssinians for forty four days before surrendering honorably. The little-known battle is depicted on the Galliano label. Golden yellow in color, sweet almost to a fault, the flowery vanilla-flavored Italian liqueur has itself laid siege to a growing number of American mixed drinks, the most famous being the Harvey Wallbanger and Golden Cadillac.

Grand Marnier An 80-proof orange liqueur with a cognac base.

Grenadine A nonalcoholic syrup made from pomegranate juice, red in color, and used to flavor and color many exotic cocktails.

Highball A generic term referring to a high eight-ounce drink consisting of one or two shots of a base liquor, filled with ice, and topped with soda or soft drink beverage, such as ginger ale or 7-Up. It contains no fruit juices and is not garnished.

Irish Mist A liqueur consisting of Irish whiskey, heather honey, and various herbal flavors. History has it that despite the feuding clans of Ireland, the secret for making this "heather wine" was never lost until Tudor armies invaded from England. Irish refugees smuggled the secret into Europe where it lay shrouded in its own mist for centuries. In the 1940s an Austrian refugee from World War II produced his family's "ancient" recipe for the mysterious brew and when tasted—begorra!—it was indeed the lost Irish Mist!

Julep A drink born in Kentucky and, according to purists, made only with Kentucky bourbon. Juleps use mint leaves, some of which are muddled in the drink for flavor and others left as sprigs for garnish. Shaved ice, frosted glasses, and straws for slow southern sippin' complete the legendary drink which in one or other of its variations is a must while watching the Kentucky Derby.

Kahlúa The granddaddy (or *abuelito*) of coffee liqueurs. Coming from Mexico, this popular brand is frequently served after dinner by itself in place of another cup of coffee. A great mixer in drinks that call for a strong, rich coffee flavor.

Kirsch or Kirschwasser Double named because of its origins in the French–German Alpine district where Germany, France, and Switzerland rub shoulders. It is a white brandy made from the fermentation of cherry pits.

Kümmel A caraway-flavored liqueur, originally made in Holland, and so enjoyed there by Peter the Great while he was traveling and working as a common laborer (disguised, of course, to learn Western ways) that he decided in order to really bring Russia into the then-modern world of the eighteenth century, the Russians must have kümmel. So he took it home with him. Since then, other northern Europeans have produced kümmel and, depending on which house and country it comes from, quality, degree of sweetness, and the varying tastes the undertone of anise will differ.

125

Lager A beer produced by bottom fermentation which means the yeast is on the bottom of the tank during fermentation, rather than on the top. Beer manufactured this way is lighter and has more sparkle than the ales and stouts that utilize the top fermentation method. Because bottom-fermented beers need some time after being bottled to mature, they should be stored for several months before being consumed. The German word for "to store" is—you guessed it!—*lager*.

Madeira A Portuguese wine made on the island of Madeira about four hundred miles off the coast of Morocco. What gives Madeira its glamor and mystique is that it is fortified with brandy and its rich flavor found its way into the homes of the very rich. The high echelon of society can still mutter the old cliché about having "some madeira, my dear," and carry it off with considerable aplomb.

Maraschino A cherry liqueur made from the black marasca cherry that at one time grew on the Dalmatian coast then ruled by Venice but which is now Yugoslavia. Redrawing political boundaries, however, did not interfere with the production of maraschino. The Italian producers carried the seed back to the Po River valley and today the famous cherry liqueur is made in both Italy and Yugoslavia.

Menthe, Crème de A sweet liqueur that comes in two colors and one flavor. The colors are mint green and white; the flavor is mint. The green mint somehow looks "right," but there is no difference between the green and white when it comes to the minty taste.

Noyaux, Crème de A pinkish almond-flavored liqueur made from the stony kernels of apricots, peaches, and other fruits. It makes an excellent after-dinner drink as well as a mixing ingredient in cocktails that call for the pithy tang of almond.

Orange Liqueur In the Dutch West Indies there is an island called Curaçao where bitter little green oranges grow. From them come the curaçao liqueurs of varying hues but similar orangey taste. Triple sec is an orange-flavored liqueur. So is Cointreau, named after its producer.

Orgeat A nonalcoholic syrup, perfect in cocktails that call for almond flavoring.

Ouzo An anise-flavored drink from Greece that is usually diluted with water and ice before drinking. Taken in its undiluted form, the licorice flavor may be truly sickening. Only small children can handle that much straight licorice and smile.

Peppermint Schnapps A minty liqueur less syrupy and sweet than crème de menthe.

Pernod The best-known substitute for the outlawed absinthe. Originally it was a brand of absinthe, but now it is the (almost) harmless anise-flavored liqueur.

Pousse-café Any after-dinner drink (the term literally means "push down the coffee") made from a variety of liqueurs of varying colors, poured carefully and according to their specific densities so that the outcome has a layered look. It takes a certain amount of skill and practice to be able to float the liqueurs on each other and then to serve the drink without the various ingredients sliding into one another.

Rickey In the family of collins and sours, the rickey is made with a liquor base, lime, cracked ice, and soda or another fizzy beverage. Served in a highball glass.

Sambuca An Italian liqueur with an anise flavor that can be served dramatically with two or three coffee beans floating on the surface. When ignited, the beans release a delicious coffee aroma. Blow it out before drinking. For a less dramatic effect, try Sambuca Negra. It is already coffee-flavored, is easily recognizable from its white brother because of its dark brown color, and requires no pyrotechnics.

Schnapps A white, hard liquor served in small glasses. In northern Europe, schnapps or (schnaps) can mean several different drinks, including ginlike drinks made with juniper berries and various brandies. Usually it is a clear grain spirit with the distinct taste of the base ingredient.

Sherry A fortified blended wine with brandy added during the fermentation process. A special type of yeast called flor is used because it can live in higher amounts of alcohol than ordinary yeast and it gives it a distinctive flavor. In spite of this, sherry is not a strong wine, usually only 15 to 18 percent alcohol.

Sloe Gin A gin with macerated sloe berries. At about 50 proof, it seems relatively harmless, but it is notorious for sneaking up on you.

Sour A versatile and much loved cocktail consisting of a base liquor shaken with lemon juice and sugar, then served either up or on the rocks.

Tia Maria A Jamaican coffee liqueur, drier than Kahlúa.

Toddy A good drink on cold days or when you have a cold. Many variations abound, but the chief ingredients are a spirit and hot water.

Triple Sec An orange liqueur from the West Indies that makes a suitable and cheaper substitute in cocktails that call for Cointreau.

INDEX